A Geomantic
Guidebook to

Water Spirits
of the World
- from nymphs to nixies,
serpents to sirens

by Alanna Moore

A Geomantic
Guidebook to

Water Spirits
of the World
- from nymphs to nixies,
serpents to sirens

by Alanna Moore

ISBN - 978-0-9757782-4-1

Published by Python Press, PO Box 929 Castlemaine 3450 Australia
Email - pythonpress@gmail.com.

Photos by the author, except for those on pages 40, 97 and 100, by Peter Cowman; by Suzy Keys on page 53; by Billy Arnold on page 115; and on page 122, courtesy of Bencherlite via Wikipedia Commons.

With thanks to Peter Cowman (desk top publishing).

Cover: Alexander Fountain, Bendigo, Victoria, Australia, featuring fabulous water nymphs and water horses.

Printed by Lightning Source.

Table of Contents

Detecting water spirits at a dowsing workshop, Esperance, Western Australia.

5

1. Introduction

Water spirits loom large in early folklore traditions globally. In later legends their shrinking importance fades into murkiness. Who are they? Do they really exist and are they still out there? Where are they found? And could it be possible for them to be recognised today?

This Geomantic Guidebook casts a fresh light on the world of water spirits, examining the mythic heritage and their roles and functions in the living landscape. It explains the energetic characterists of these other-dimensional devic beings, while exploring some of the many sacred site, water spirit hot spots of the world.

The author has been a dowser and geomancer for over 30 years. Her studies of the nature spirits in indigenous folklore (Australian, Maori and Irish in particular) have shown that grains of wisdom have been passed down through the ages, often thinly disguised in order to escape waves of cultural genocide, and kept alive by the Irish seanachies and Aboriginal and Maori lore holders. Her energetic mapping of landscapes in Australia, New Zealand, Ireland and elsewhere has confirmed many of those precious grains of truth.

Lifting the shrouds of mystery from ancient animist paradigms of the spiritual reality of nature and the esoteric importance of water in the landscape, the book follows on from an earlier one by the author (The Wisdom of Water, 2007). Delving more deeply into water's spirit, it spotlights spiritual traditions of the past and rare accounts of modern encounters with water spirits by the author today. It encourages greater understanding of and closer connection with the devic dimensions of water. And it gives suggestions for how one may develop the ability to find and meaningfully connect with the spirits of water oneself.

2. Who are the devas
and spirits of water?

The spirits of nature, also known as devas (from the Indian word deva, meaning shining one), personify the spiritual reality of nature. Dismissed by many as imaginary, they are actually an other-dimensional kingdom of life, a society of conscious beings. Observed by clairvoyants in various sizes, shapes and colours, they are detected by dowsing as spherical fields of consciousness. Devas exhibit vitality, emotion and intelligence. They reproduce, live and die (fading away, they are re-absorbed into the ether) and they also evolve, just as the rest of nature does. They interact with the flora and fauna, and assist its development and evolution; and they interact with the human world as well. The totemic spirits of Aboriginal Australia are good examples of the intimate bonds forged between devas and some human societies.

Devas are shape shifters. They are composed of energetic matter, generally corresponding to the etheric and astral type matter recognised in the human energy field. To clairvoyant vision they can manifest in any shape that suits them, displaying their favourite guises in order to be better recognised. Often they choose to look like the dominant animals of the local environment, such as the two big waterfall spirits that the author observed in Malaysian jungle in May 2011 - their visual forms were of big king-kong-like orang utans!

The energetic forms (devic fields) may be quite condensed at times, while at other times they can spread out over a much larger area. Some are found dwelling in the Earth, or in water, air or fire; these devas are often referred to as elemental beings. But they don't necessarily always stay fixed to their elemental domains.

Highly evolved devas have influence over large areas and harmony on

8

Earth is all the better maintained when these locally important devas are happy and undisturbed. In many cases the effect of human veneration of important nature spirits has been to empower and accelerate their development, and over time these have gained elevated status. Thus a region's devas became the gods and goddesses of early tribal nations. In Ireland and Britain tribal identification with a goddess was an early form of nationalism. For example the Irish had Eriu for their tutelary deity, and, in earlier times, Danu/Danaan ruled the Tuatha da Danaan; while the British had Brit (Brigantia, Britannia).

The mythic gods provided prototypes, models of human behaviour for people to emulate, archetypes to inhabit the collective consciousness of mankind. Thus mother goddesses, for example, exemplified the maternal warmth, compassion, protectiveness and fortitude required to rear children; while war goddesses were powerful protectors of sovereignty. The gods influenced human society, while also being somewhat a product of it. Thus these highly evolved spiritual beings evolved over time, to reflect changing environments and regimes.

Mythic oral traditions were constantly altering to suit the fashion of the times, often the status of some deities was downgraded and they were later portrayed as merely ancestor heroes, demi-gods, demons or fairies - shadows of their former selves. But devas of all types are still out there at large and they can easily be perceived, by attunement and dowsing. Anyone genuinely interested can develop the ability to connect into their consciousness and perceive them in their haunts.

Spirits of Water

Indigenous peoples have long attributed sanctity to the waters of the planet, with water divinities highly respected. Their presence was recognised and honoured in bubbling springs, brooks, bogs, rivers, wetlands, waterfalls, oceans, pools and lakes. They were known to exhibit dynamic fluidity - living underground in watery depths, inhabiting vast oceans and marshlands, and also capable of rising up into the air in mist or fog; with some able to inhabit either or all of these locations at various times.

Spirits of water were generally revered above all the other elemental beings, for many had special relationships with humankind. Naidies, for example, are the Greco-Roman spirits of sacred pools and springs, and they were considered the patrons of music and poetry. The Muses are another inspirational species of water spirit, also associated with sacred springs, but more highly evolved than the Naidies. Chief god Apollo ruled over the Muses.

If we muse upon something we reflect, gaze, silently meditate, until understanding or inspiration flows. The idea of water being a source of creative intelligence is global. In one old Irish tale it was mentioned that *"the poets thought it was always on the brink of water (that) poetry was revealed to them"*.

Divine feminine

Divine water beings were often personified as beautiful females, such as flirty, fertile nymphs associated with this well or that spring. Under Christian influence, people would sometimes encounter a solemn 'lady of the lake' or a saintly 'woman in white'.

The most highly evolved spiritual dimension of water, its heart and soul, might be simply referred to as the Spirit of Water. Traditionally personified as a pre-eminent divine feminine being, She is a compassionate, creative, benevolent motherly figure, whose spiritual continuum could never be fully extinguished by Christianity and other religions. Not only did She rule life, but often death and rebirth as well. In pagan Greece, for example, nature goddess Artemis ruled over waterways and She delighted in spinning, weaving and circle dancing with the Naidies.

The Spirit of Water has survived culturally today by taking on the guise of the Biblical Mary and She now answers to that name. Mother Mary type presences are typically seen cloaked in colour combinations of white, silver and blue. She can manifest anywhere and everywhere, typically at or near a water feature, and also using other names and forms. But in waters that have been fouled, Her spirit may be absent.

Below: Golden votive offerings found in a sacred spring in England (British Museum). The deity on the left apppears to be sovreignty goddess Britannia. The figure on the right, perhaps a goddess of fertility. Interestingly, she stands on a serpent which could be representing her mastery of the Earth forces, harking back to sacred serpent deities of more ancient times. This intriguing figure is reminiscent of similar images found globally, including those of the Virgin Mary from the Catholic tradition (see page 57) and Kuan Yin from the east, where the divine female being is also sometimes depicted standing on a serpent /dragon being.

3. Amphibious creators and storm gods

In the creation myths of many cultures from Neolithic times, gods and goddesses emerged from the waters as primary creators, or brought with them the know-how to kick-start or advance human culture. Water or storm deities were often the sacred ancestors, creators and law makers in the earliest of cultures.

Often the gods were depicted in a half fish/half human form. Ea, for example, was one of a trinity of Babylonian creator gods based in the primordial ocean that surrounded and supported the mythic Earth. Part human, part fish (or sometimes described as a fish-tailed goat), He was a god of fresh waters, wisdom, magic and oracular powers.

In Greece, an early creation myth recorded by Athenagoras in the 2nd century says that in the beginning there was water. From it emerged a snake with three heads, that of a lion, a bull and a giant, Herakles or Kronos, who went on to create an egg, which split in two to create heaven and Earth. (Maria Gimbutas suggests it was originally a horned snake that emerged first from the waters.)

Storm gods

Most of the leading Indo-European gods originally ruled the sky, from whence they bestowed rain and Earthly fertility, generally using lightning as their deadly weapon. Often weather/sky god and goddess pairs ruled the cosmic roost, their many children becoming the lesser deities. Though usually considered male, in Russia and Lithuania the thunder god, Perperuna and Percuna Tete, is female and a Mother of Thunder.

Baal, the Canaanite (western Semitic) god of death and rebirth, is a typical storm god. He resides on Sapan Mountain and is depicted wielding thunderbolts, His voice is the thunder. He is also associated with Earthly fertility and has an underworld connection too. Aspects of God in the Bible seem to have been borrowed from this thunder god. Zeus/Jupiter became the leading sky god of the Greeks and Romans. Jupiter, in His thundering guise, was called Fulgar, the name later chosen for objects created by lightning. Virile Zeus, who sired a vast number of other deities, dispensed justice and thunderbolts forged by the one-eyed Cyclopes. Athenians prayed to Him for rain during droughts, especially at Mount Lycaeus, Zeus' birthplace, where there was a sacred spring dedicated to Him.

Zeus' totems are the eagle and the Oak. Oak is known as an attractor of lightning. Oak trees like to grow over underground water streams, so it's not surprising they 'court the flash' and that people traditionally never shelter under them during electrical storms. At his famous, and the most ancient, oracle centre at Dodona, where a sacred spring arose from beneath an Oak tree, Zeus' oracular messages, heard in the gurgling of water and rustling of leaves, were interpreted by His priests and priestesses. (It has been suggested that Zeus evolved originally from an Oak tree spirit.)

The Baltic storm god Perkunas/Perkons, depicted as a red-bearded, axe-carrying man who drives His billy-goat drawn chariot across the sky, is another dispenser of justice. He sends thunderbolts to evildoers.

It was also said that *"the first thunderbolt in spring purified the Earth and encouraged growth,"* writes Sheena McGrath. Perkunas was also a warrior and blacksmith. In Prussia Perkunas temples had eternal flames tended by virgin maidens and only Oak wood was burned there.

Axes were popular with storm gods. Images of axes in the petroglyphs of Sweden and eastern Europe probably represent the storm god Thor. (The axe later evolved into a hammer, the god becoming a smith, a master of forging with fire and water.) One of the huge stones of Stonehenge in England has a faint axe carved onto it.

And in Aboriginal northern Australia the Lightning Man, Namarakon, (pictured below) wears stone axes on his knees and elbows, and hurls them to make thunder.

We now know that lightning can fix atmospheric nitrogen and thus make it available via rain for plants, so the ancient connection between lightning and fertility proves to be correct.

If we add to the fact that lightning can actually create amino acids, the building blocks of life, it seems that our ancestors had intuited the important functions that electrical storms and rain have provided to the nourishment and development of life on Earth, if not, perhaps, to its very existence.

Aboriginal rock painting of lightning spirit
Namarrakon, in Kakadu National Park,
Northern Territory, Australia.

4. Serpent spirits

Sacred Serpent – Spirit of Wisdom

Probably the oldest lineage of creator deities is that of the great water serpent spirits. With sinuous and sensuous forms they are often likened to non-venomous snakes, especially pythons, who are masters of their environment, capable of swimming the waters, diving into holes in the ground and climbing up high into trees.

The sacred serpent also came to represent the endless cycles of life, of life, death and rebirth, no doubt from its ability to shed its skin, and also from the fact that it often hibernates each winter, to emerge in spring. This principle has been represented by the image of the serpents egg and recurring creation/immortality symbols of the giant snake circle of the universe, its tail in its mouth. This archetypal symbol is still seen today, as an emblem used both by the Theosophical Society and also the permaculture movement, where it represents wisdom and the natural cycles of fertility, rejuvenation and sustainability.

Sacred serpents have long been associated with the gaining of esoteric wisdom and Theosophist visionary Geoffrey Hodson described this beautifully in 1977 when he said that:

'The serpent is the symbol of wisdom because wisdom glides unseen everywhere, seeking entry into the mind of man; the serpent glides through the forest and the fields, silent, certain of its way.

'Receive it rightly and it will illumine. Misuse it and it will sting. Do not attack the serpent. Be still and it will glide near you, and you will see its movement and its beauty. Its venom will either destroy or heal.'

From earliest times snake gods and goddesses are found in all corners of the world. While many evolved over time into different forms with divergent functions, generally they represent and rule over the waters of the Earth. For example Yam or Jamm, the Phoenician god of seas and waters in general, whose gilded bronze image has a snake wrapped around the upper torso; and perhaps the beautiful snake goddess of the Minoans, in ancient Crete, the location said by some to be the 'Atlantis' of legend.

On the local level, a multitude of lesser snake spirits that inhabit the waters are often explained as being the chief deities' offspring. Temples and altars to snake deities often have snakes not only depicted in art, sometimes the real thing lives there too. There are several snake temples in India and elsewhere where living snakes rule the roost!

Serpents in Africa

Serpent deities are common in Africa, where they no doubt presided over the earliest of traditions. There the great horned serpent being, Aido Hwedo, also known as Ouroboros, represents the whole universe, as it coils inside a great calabash biting it's own tail, a symbol of eternity and the endless cycles of birth, death and rebirth.

In the Kalahari, Bushmen say that horned serpent beings around 10m (32 ft) long are the guardians of water holes. In Zimbabwe giant serpents spirits reach up to 30km long. Zimbabwean legends speak of a creator snake spirit who carried mountains and men on its back. A rock painting from the Matopo Hills, now in the Bulawayo museum, depicts a primordial python from which all other animals emerge. In Venda tradition the whole of creation sat inside the belly of the Python, which vomited them into existence. Yet another serpent around Matopo, the 12ft/3.6m long Muhlambela, was said to have the call of an antelope, while its feathered head is a feature of similar serepent deities the world over.

Though usually associated with landscape waters, Africa's water serpent deities were also considered Masters of the Forest, as is one

Mombo-wa-Ndlopfu. Horned rainbow snakes, such as a famous one called Likongoro, do prefer to live in water, but when they go onto land they can shape shift to other animal forms. Horse and antelope-headed water snake spirits are common in Africa. These sometimes have a connection with shooting stars and the horse-headed ones are sometimes depicted with stars shining on their foreheads. There are also bird and human-headed snake deities, while hairy hippopotamus / snake beings are referred to as water horses.

Gigantic serpents give their name to the Drakensburg or Dragon Mountains of South Africa. Inkanyamba, who dwells at the summit of Mount Mpendle, is one, a rain bringer who, Le Quellec was told, travels from mountain to mountain in order to *"copulate in water bodies"*.

In the Vodun traditions of West Africa, Rainbow Serpent Dan (also called Dambala or Dangbe) is the god of wealth and co-creator of the world, a python deity responsible for regulating the weather and agricultural fecundity. Dan transported primary god Mawu-Lisa through the universe as it was being created. Dan's shrines are often decorated with a snake-headed rainbow. Since those legendary creation times, Dan has been coiled in a spiral around the Earth, keeping things together and manifesting in the presence of rainbows and in light reflected in water.

Kings of West African kingdoms in southern Benin created sinuous encircling earthworks of ditchs and banks around their palace complexes. These invoked sacred protection and the royal family walked them on their annual processions to the Dangba temples, which were presided over by sacred pythons who lived there in the lap of luxury. Serpentine ditches are still used today to represent the Rainbow Serpent in Vodun rites, derived from African religion, that are practised in Haiti.

O'duda is a West African mother goddess whose name means The Black One and Her image is the serpent. Popular in Santeria tradition, derived from Nigerian Yoruba culture, in the Caribbean she is referred to as Saint Claire.

In Egypt

In Egypt serpent deities are also ubiquitious. Some are destroyers and some protectors. Serpents are depicted accompanying the recently deceased on their journey to the underworld in a sacred boat.

Certain winged serpents symbolise the gods and goddesses. Nehebu-Kau is a goddess of the underworld and the great snake upon which the world rests. Wadjet, an important snake goddess of southern Egypt, is depicted as a cobra about to strike. Renenutet, another cobra goddess, is appealed to for a bountiful harvest and easy childbirth.

Egypt's earliest creation story features a serpent and the primordial egg, which contains the 'Bird of Light'. Apep (Apepi or Apophis) is the cosmic serpent of chaos and destruction that lives in the dark underworld. As in similar myths elsewhere, each night he lies waiting to ambush sun god Ra as He travels by ship along the celestial Nile--in-the-sky, the Milky Way.

The sun's return each morning is celebrated as a triumph of life over death. Ra is the father of Shu, god of air, and Tefnut, goddess of moisture. His tears formed the first humans. In a painting in the Papyrus of Huefer (kept in the British Museum) the Great Cat, a very ancient solar deity, it's cult centred in Heliopolis, is shown slaying the serpent Apepi, its enemy, at the foot of the Sacred Tree.

Snakes and trees are often associated together in religious imagery from India to Scandinavia. Their sacred powers and the cyclic interplay of sun (or fire) and water are likewise recurring themes in many of the world's traditions.

Egyptian pharoahs wore the Ureaus snake on their foreheads, at the 'third eye', brow chakra position, as a symbol of power, wisdom, and the firey kundalini force that flows up the spine.

*Sacred serpents and snakey deities
in artworks feature from ancient times. (British Museum).*

19

5. Serpent spirits of Mesopotamia and the Bible

Serpentine deities are often described in dragon-like forms in the ancient mythology of Mesopotamia. Tiamat is the ferocious female dragon ruling chaos and the primordial oceans. Tiamat is also the Babylonian name for the sea (a grammatically feminine name). Together with male god Apsu, ruler of the fresh waters, these two deities were the parents of all the other gods.

They also spawned a fearsome collection of monsters including horned serpents and giant snakes described in the clay tablets of the Epic of Creation as ferocious dragons *"cloaked with fearsome rays...bearing mantles of radiance"*. Tiamat later fought with the other gods. On one level such events represent the battles of the seasonal cycles, the annual storms of winter and dangers lurking in the deep seas.

Tiamat battled with the future chief water god Ea and then His son Marduk, who eventually killed Her and split Her body in two. From each half of Her body, Marduk made the heavens and Earth, the Earth half being responsible for keeping out the subterranean waters below.

He later killed Her son too and mixed his blood with soil to create humankind. Marduk pierced Tiamat's eyes to create the sources of the rivers Tigris and Euphrates; and he bent Her tail up into the sky to form the Milky Way.

The Sumerians worshipped Ninhursag or Nintu – as 'She who gave birth'. This creator goddess was typically depicted as a snake or a human form with a fish tail. Other Babylonian deities were also depicted in serpent form and these were all equally capable of good and bad deeds.

The Serpent in the Bible

Christian and Jewish traditions absorbed and reinvented much of the pre-existing mythologies of their times, often retelling tales that chronicled the changing fashion in deities and cults. Thus in the Bible's Old Testament we find Leviathan, a ferocious serpent-dragon of a sea monster, no doubt based on old Tiamat. In the Bible's Isaiah, Leviathan is referred to as the 'crooked serpent'.

We have more hints of the legend's origins in the late 5th century Babylonian Talmud, where Leviathan is said to have been 'created on the fifth day' with all the other fishes, becoming a plaything of God. The Talmud contains references to male and female Leviathans, as well as to God killing a female one.

In the Pesikta de Rab Kahana, a text from around the 7th century, the fins of Leviathan *"radiate such brilliant light as to obscure the light of the sun"*. Clearly there was going to be a problem of competition here, in the new monotheistic religion!

Greek and Sumerian Edens were paradises that feature sacred trees of life and knowledge. These usually harbour oracular serpents, wise ones who guide mankind and guard secrets of immortality. In the Judeo-Christian tradition, however, the serpent became the personification of the enemy. Leviathan came to be cast as absolute evil and the Devil was said to manifest in serpent form. The demonised serpent remains one of the foremost metaphors for evil in the Western World and many people hold irrational fears about snakes, as well.

Clues to explain the abhorrence of the serpent come from Hebrew legends that describe Leviathan as the child of Adam's first wife Lilith. Often depicted with wings and the body of a snake, Lilith was deemed to be the temptress of Eve in the Garden of Eden, some say. Her name means storm goddess and the Owl, a symbol of wisdom, was Her sacred animal.

Lillith (British Museum).

The serpent in the Biblical story represented a personification of the old goddess cults that were so anathema to patriarchal Christianity. Author Mary Condren says that the original Eve was also depicted as a serpent and that her earlier name Hawwah means serpent as well as 'mother of all living things' in many Semitic languages.

In the Old Testament, Leviathan appears in Psalms 74:14 as a terrifying multiheaded sea serpent, *"the king of all wild beasts"*, that is killed by God and given as food to the Hebrews in the wilderness. This probably depicts the Hebrew campaign to wipe out pagan goddess cults, reflecting a patriarchal take-over of the indigenous culture, suggests Barbara Walker.

In Mesopotamia, as in Egypt, the serpent symbolised life, its creation and regeneration. Once elevated as all-wise, the serpent became an impediment to later religious cults. Demonising anything to do with it was striking a blow at paganism's persistence.

6. Serpent spirits in India and the Americas

Hinduism in India incorporates the animistic world-view and serpent beings, called nagas, are recognized as highly important deities in the devic hierarchies there. Nagas are recognised as guardians of Earth's treasures and bringers of fertility. Nagarajas (queen and king nagas) are responsible for rainfall and waterways. They also protect against fires caused by lightning. In spring they climb into the sky and in winter they go down to live deep within the Earth.

Nagas are depicted in human, half human and fully serpent forms. Sometimes multiple headed, they are also associated with various other gods. Shiva is often seen wearing snakes around his neck and arms, or with the naga Vasuki as a girdle. This same serpent, also called Shesha, was used as a rope to churn the primordial ocean. And when Vishnu rests, it is on top of a nagaraja. (This is reminiscent of Mary in Catholic iconography, when she is sometimes depicted standing on a serpent.)

Snake goddesses feature strongly in the south of India, which is not surprising, as African people migrated directly there in earliest times. In Bengal, Manasa is the primary snake goddess and a ruler of agriculture. A giver and protector of children, and promoter of wealth and wellbeing, she is invoked to save devotees from snake bite.

Mariyamman is the best known snake goddess in Tamil Nadu. A goddess of rain and protector of the people, she is worshipped in snake and also tree forms. (The root word *mari*, from the Sanskrit, Mary in English, is applied to all things marine.)

Nagas are invoked at the Nagapanchami festival, held at the start of the rainy season in August, especially by those hoping to be blessed with children. In southern India women desiring children erect snake stones under sacred trees. The stones are carved with stylised cobras to represent the Goddess Nakamal, the snake virgin. These are first immersed in water for several months to empower them and are then ritually placed under sacred Neem or Pipal trees.

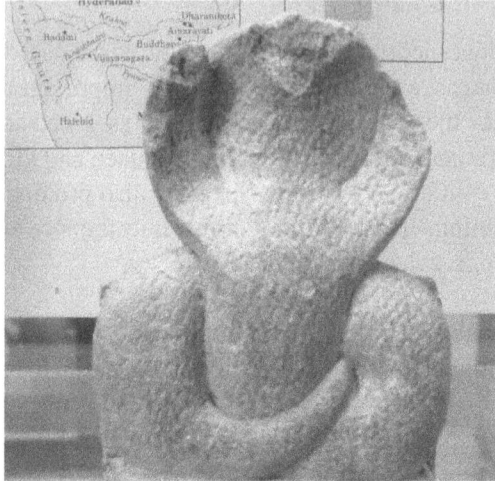

Sacred cobra statue from India (British Museum).

In later Buddhist tradition, nagas are water deities guarding Buddhist texts. The task of guarding one particular sutra teaching (the Prajnaparamita of Mahayana) was assigned by Buddha to the nagas, but only until such a time as when mankind is ready to receive it (which hasn't happened yet).

Buddha was said to have been protected from a downpour by the seven headed nagaraja Mucilinda, who sheltered him with its outstretched hoods over seven days. A 3rd century AD stone Buddha statue depicts Mucilinda coiled beneath the Buddha as he sits under the sacred fig tree at Bodh-Gaya.

In the Hindu island of Bali we find nagas also (pictured next page), as well as legends of Antaboga the world serpent, a being who was present at the beginning of time and who created the world turtle Bedawang through his meditation. On top of Bedawang lies another two snakes and a Black Stone, lid to the underworld.

*Balinese
temple nagas*

Serpents in central America

In Meso-America the serpent is seen in religious art from earliest recorded times, with images from the Olmec pre-classic era of 1150-500 BCE. The famous Olmec stone heads, with typical African negroid features, are possible pointers to the cult's African influences. And, as in Europe, India, Egypt and many other places, hybrid snake/bird and snake/human forms of major deities are also found in this region.

Quetzalcoatl (also called Gukumatz, Nine Wind and Kukulcan) is the pre-eminent feathered or plumed serpent god revered by Olmec, Mixtec, Toltec, Aztec and Mayan peoples, and from whom almost all Meso-American peoples claim descent.

The ancient city of Teotihuacan was dedicated both to water god Tlaloc and also Quetzalcoatl, his subordinate, as representations of the fertility of the Earth. As Quetzalcoatl's cult evolved he became responsible for the rain, the celestial waters and winds, while Tlaloc ruled the Earthly waters and vegetation.

The Maya regarded Quetzalcoatl as a being who would transport the gods, while the Nahuas considered him an originator of the arts, poetry and all knowledge. The Aztec turned him into a symbol of dying and resurrection and made him a patron of their priesthood.

In some rural parts of Mexico today there is still the belief that in certain caves lives a great feathered snake that can only be seen by special people. To ensure plentiful rain it must be placated. The feathered serpent is also worshipped by Huichol and Cora Indians to this day.

Quetzalcoatl and the 'end of time'

The Pyramid of Kukulcan at Chichen-Itza is a superb and highly accurate time-keeping device of impressive astronomical accuracy. It's ancient astronomer priests were able to determine the exact alignment of the Earth, the Sun, the star cluster Pleiades and the center of our Galaxy that will take place on December 21st 2012, explains Hector Carreon. He goes to say that:

"On this date, according to the Mayans and subsequent Meso-American civilizations, the return of Kukulcan (Quetzalcoatl) will take place. As the Sun sets west of Chichen-Itza, a pattern of shadow and light will project the Plumed Serpent (Quetzalcoatl) descending the stairs of the pyramid that has a large head of a serpent sculpted in rock at the base. This occurs twice in Chichen Itza every year but on the Winter Solstice of December 21, 2012 something very special will happen. As the Sun sets in the early afternoon, the shadow of the pyramid's northwest edge will project a moving pattern of light that joins and illuminates the sculpted serpent head at the base of the stairway. Within a thirty-four minute period, the serpent, formed by this play of light and shadow will appear to descend to the Earth, as the sun leaves each stair, going from the top to the bottom. This combined effect creates the visual appearance of the body of the serpent descending the pyramid, (while)...the tail of the serpent projected up from the top of the pyramid will be pointing precisely to the Pleiades."

Serpents in North America

Further north in the Americas feathered or bearded serpents are found in the Pueblo Indian lore of Arizona and New Mexico; while Hopi Indians still perform snake dances. Cherokee people revere Uktena, a large and powerful horned serpent being. Fearsome, but rain bringing, Thunderbird spirits of various North American legends are continually battling with horned serpents and other monsters of the deep, resulting in earthquakes, floods and thunderstorms.

Near Peebles, Ohio, lies the famous Great Serpent Mound, a massive earthwork depicting a curving snake with what looks like an egg in its mouth (otherwise thought to depict a snake with head reared and about to bite) and ending with a triple coiled tail. This is the world's largest effigy mound, at 1,333ft/440m long and up to 3ft/1m high. It is also surrounded by several smaller burial mounds nearby.

Long a mystery, its age is guessed to be between 1000 - 2000 years old. Older still, by some 500 years, are the serpent mounds found further north in Canada. This suggests that snake cults originally came overland from Asia, when there was a connecting land bridge, to infuse their way southwards.

Archeo-astronomical examination of the Great Serpent Mound reveals that the head area is aligned to the summer solstice sunset, while its coils align with the winter solstice sunrise, the autumnal and spring equinox sunrises, and the summer solstice sunrise. Also discovered are a remarkable array of lunar alignments associated with the same coils, indicating a familiarity of designers with long lunar cycles. The Great Serpent Mound may also have been designed to be a mirror of the Draconis (Draco) constellation, from the time of the highest position of the north star, Draconis-alpha (Thuban), some think.

Interestingly, crop circles have been appearing in the vicinity of the Great Serpent Mound for several years, the American Society of

Dowsers Journal reported in its Winter 2004 edition. One striking design, the 'All-Seeing Eye' reported by dowser Delsey Knoechelman in August 2003, was found to be in alignment with the coiled tail of the nearby Great Serpent and connected to it by a dowseable energy line. Around the time of its appearance there were reports of mysterious aerial lights, including a dark orange sphere seen at night.

Knoechelman described how, at the end of every crop circle dowsing expedition, Doug McIlwain performed a Native American 'Four Winds' ceremony within the circle, using cornmeal, sage and tobacco in a medicine wheel design. After doing this at the 'All-Seeing Eye', he reported that it: *"brought about a strong, breezy magnetic/electric field effect which caused a tingling in the body. It also caused the temperature of the crop circles to rise about 20 degrees Fahrenheit so that the auric field was palpable. Astonishingly, people came to warm their hands over the medicine wheel design, which seemed to hold an invisible fire. This Indian magic was a true marvel and outside my previous realm of possibilities."*.

Curious landscape phenomena, such as crop circles and 'Earth lights' are typically more prevalent in highly faulted or volcanic country. Not surprisingly, the location of the Great Serpent Mound is likewise highly significant. Found to be at the convergence of three distinctly different soil types, it is also situated on top of an unique geological structure of faulted and folded bedrock, usually found as a result of a meteorite or a volcanic explosion. This crypto-explosion structure was a great mystery until 2003, when researchers concluded that a meteorite strike was responsible. They were able to date the meteorite impact to the Permian Period, around 248 to 286 million years ago.

Analysis of the form and function of this earth mound by researcher Miroslav Provod finds that its meandering serpent shape creates high energy zones, especially on the inner bends. Likewise for the inner bends of rivers. Provod relates that: *"The burial-ground of the rulers of Egypt, the Kings Valley, is situated in a meander of the River Nile."*. Ireland's famed Newgrange complex is also located in the inner bend of sacred river, the Boyne, he adds.

7. Chinese snakes
and dragons

In China serpentine dragons are ubiquitous in the mythic landscape and sky heavens. Chinese dragons rule waters both above and below the ground, and are equally at home swimming in watery depths as they are flying up into the clouds to make it rain.

Serpents in Chinese creation myths are remarkably similar to Egyptian legends. One of the earliest versions has an archaic goddess called Woman Gua (Nu Gua), gua meaning snail like creature. Depicted with a human upper torso and snake tail, it was She who made the cosmos and all living beings. Humans She created from mud baked in Her oven; black people being the more well cooked ones.

In later myths Nu Gua is linked with a male culture hero, another half snake god, Fu Xi, translated as Prostrate (Sacrificial) Victim, who invented writing, divination and hunting technologies. As the first divine married couple, their tails tenderly entwined, they are depicted holding their emblems, Hers the compass, His, the carpenter's square (later, these pop up as potent symbols of western Freemasonry).

In another classic myth, the giant being Pan Gu (meaning Coiled Antiquity) is the first born semi-divine human, a child of Yin and Yang who emerged from the primordial chaos out of a cosmic egg and became responsible for the weather.

When Pan Gu died his breath became the clouds and wind, his eyes – the sun and moon, limbs – the mountains, head hair – the stars, flesh – the soil, and body hair – vegetation, while his body fluids became the rain and rivers. Thus he gave his body for the benefit of mankind and this archetypal story is an early version of the universal myth of the annual growth and death of the vegetation god.

Dragon rock, Chinese Gardens, Sydney

Chinese dragons

China's water dragons govern the weather, tides and water levels. Originally thought of as rain deities that live in lakes and rivers, they were regularly invoked in times of drought. The Dragon Dance still vigorously performed at Chinese New Year festivities was originally a ritual of rain making.

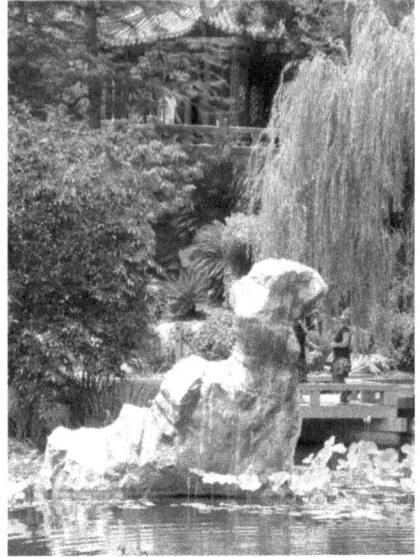

To bring rain, water dragons fly up to the clouds and, when contented, they ensure the fertility of the fields and the prosperity of the people. Water is synonymous with money and success in China; while the geomantic art of feng shui literaly translates as 'wind and water'.

Although fearsome adversaries, Chinese dragons are generally regarded as auspicious beasts, protectors who guard treasures, waterways, clouds and winds, and even Heaven itself. In drought times their images were taken from the temples to show the dragon the damage done and to encourage precipitation.

If water dragons are interfered with, havoc can be unleashed. One should never build anything over a well (the dragon's 'eye'), or a spring (the dragon's 'ear'). It would be seriously bad feng shui! Storms are considered to be battling dragons, droughts are sleeping dragons and floods are wrathful ones.

Flooding was frequently a big problem in ancient China and resident dragons would be called upon in flood times. An imperial edict of 1869 gave thanks for an impending flood that had been averted, citing that:

"when the dykes of the Yellow River were in danger of collapse the repeated apparition of the Golden Dragon saved the day".

As for dragon lines, the lung mei of Chinese feng shui, these are energetic flows occasionally found meandering through the landscape, having emanated from an Earth chakra point, an upward spiralling energy vortex. The serpentine lines can act as pathways for local dragon spirits, helping to convey them through the air, land or water, both over and under the ground, and in the process spreading their vitalising forces throughout the land.

Generally speaking Chinese water dragons are said to live underwater for half of the year, after which they rise into the sky at springtime, when the constellation of the Dragon is at its height. New Year celebrations also welcome in the season of spring, with ceremonies to awaken the dragon forces.

The mightiest dragons of them all were said to be the sovereigns of the five oceans. Like the naga kings of India, they live in glistening crystal palaces beneath the sea.

Taiwanese dragon on a Taoist temple.

8. Dragons and serpents of Europe

Numerous images of snakes and snake goddesses, dating from the Paleolithic to Classical eras, attest to the mythic importance of the serpent across Europe. In some of the earliest art, on cave walls at Porto Badisco in Apulia, Portugal, for instance, are snake spirals and a seething mass of snake and hybrid snake/human forms painted in black.

In Scandinavia, where pagan traditions flourished much later than in most of the rest of Europe, a world serpent was said to live secured in the depths of the sea. In the Creation Song in the poem Beowulf, the cosmos is represented as a mighty World Tree (Yggdrasil) that lies in the centre of a round disc surrounded by an ocean.

Swedish dragons (Stockholm Museum).

Beneath the tree is a sacred spring and a great serpent or dragon called Nidhogg, which lies coiled beneath its roots, curled around the circle.

In England certain Bronze Age monuments follow serpentine winding pathways and standing stones at Avebury were interpreted as a serpent temple by antiquarian William Stukely in the 17th century. In the stone avenues and circles he saw the form of a three mile long snake, its head symbolised by a stone circle known as The

Sanctuary. Much later (in the late 1980's) Hamish Miller dowsed The Sanctuary and found it to be a node point (crossing) of the so-called 'Michael and Mary' Earth energy lines which traverse the breadth of the country. (I call such things - dragon lines.)

In Herefordshire a circa 4000 year old track of fire-cracked stones following a serpentine path was uncovered in 2007. The possibly 400 metre long track is aligned with the midsummer sunset and possibly the midwinter sunrise also. Unique in Britain and Europe as well, it has been dubbed the Rotherwas Ribbon and the Dinedor Serpent.

Despite it's uniqueness an access road has been allowed to be built over it by Herefordshire Council. Fear of the serpent, perhaps?

The Serpent in Greece

In Greece the god of healing, Aesculapius, is represented by a staff of intertwined snakes, a prototype still used to represent the medical profession and known as the Caduceus. At his healing temple in Epidaurus patients once slept on bare ground surrounded by snakes, in expectation of the god visiting them in dreams to prescribe cures.

Greek serpent spirits sometimes had curious, but familiar, appendages. *"A carving of the Aesculapian Serpent, as the god is known, is shown on a carving at Pompei,"* writes Holiday, *"and is unlike anything known to herpetologists. It had vertical humps and snail-like horns, exactly like the monsters in Scotland and Ireland."*

The pre-eminent serpent spirit in Greece was Python, daughter of Ge, the Earth Mother, who once ruled the sacred oracle centre at Delphi, until Apollo (god of healing, prophecy and music) speared Her. At its peak, around 2,500 years ago, Delphi's seer priestesses, known as Pythia, were consulted by individuals from far and wide and for important matters of state. Oracular rituals were centred around several sacred springs there. These were also said to be the haunt of the Muse.

European dragons

Over time the original serpentine deities of Europe became more usually depicted as dragons, gigantic eels or worms, typically found in watery landscapes, although they also ventured beyond. These slithery beings could glide sinuously through the land, or travel in the air via the aerial leys (also known as ley lines), as well as access their underworld homes via the portal points of wells and springs.

Not usually malevolent, great fury could be unleashed if their territory was disturbed. Some expected regular offerings of tribute from mankind and grew greedy. These ones could get rather prickly at times, especially if not 'fed' regularly. (As energy is their fuel, they enjoyed extracting the energetic essence of food offerings.) But otherwise they resided in the land, usually happily minding their own business.

Many were regarded as guardians, protecting underground or underwater treasures. Sometimes winged dragons were said to live coiled up at the bottom of the occasional well. Others flew from castle to castle in straight lines, the castles perhaps located on a previous sacred site and connected by linear energy leys.

In Wales the Wyvern is a two legged dragon, while a red dragon or 'water horse' features as the Welsh emblem. The Loch Ness 'monster' may be a relation. Judging by the large number of water dragon legends, there must have been quite a large population of these beings.

Confusion exists as to whether the legendary characters are merely spirits, or real flesh and blood. Viewing them as the chief spirits of waterways, sources and wetlands, their sustenance would have been the energetic essences of nature and their activities of a purely energetic kind. There is also the possibility that remnant populations of ancient life forms are the source of some sightings. Certainly, spirits of water are perceivable by clairvoyant observation, while the art of dowsing has revealed to the author their presence throughout the world.

Dragon killers in Europe

In medieval Europe, Christian propagandists bragged of saints and heroes subjugating dragons in popular dragon killing legends. But they are obviously inventions. Saint George, for example, lived in Turkey and came to be associated with dragon killing in Britain, despite the fact that he never even visited there. The legendary site of the event is said to be at Dragon Hill near Uffington, at a spot just below the eye of the Uffington White Horse, a huge and ancient figure cut into the underlying chalk. Perhaps this sacred horse figure, with its flowing lines, is actually meant to represent a dragon, some suggest.

Often in the dragon killing legends the 'beasts' were dispatched near ancient mounds (which they apparently liked to coil themselves around) and also beside standing stones. Clearly they were identified with power centres in the landscape. The hill top siting of St Michael churches (Michael being another dragon killer) was probably another form of symbolic usurption of the old Earth mystery cults.

Earlier in Greece, Apollo moved into the Temple of Delphi and the mercurial Python spirit was speared into submission by him, heralding a new religious order. As a gesture of Earth acupuncture thus performed, an omphalos stone was erected on the spot. Thus the serpent powers of Earth Mother Ge were symbolically placed beneath Apollo's control, although he was said to have done seven years penance for this.

Time after time around the world, the rule of the water serpents and dragons is mythically challenged or overcome, usually by solar heroes and sun gods. Horus killed Aphophis, Krishna killed Anatha, Marduk overcame Tiamat, Canaan's Baal did in Yamm, Heracles battled the Hydra. Perhaps they allude to the ending of the Piscean Age and the eternal battle/interplay of yin and yang: dark underworld versus bright upper world, sun and water, positive and negative forces.

Feminist authors suggest that many of these myths represent the demise of goddess based religions and herald the coming of new waves of patriarchal Indo-European tribes, such as the Celtic warrior cultures. As well as political hype, the myths speak strongly of the powers of raw nature and mankind's civilising influence over nature's chaos.

The cycles of seasonal change and renewal, and the recycling of myths to explain the planet's powers, are all represented here. And those dynamic spiritual beings, I've found, really do inhabit the other dimensions of reality; their enduring consciousness is the other part of the equation.

Dragons surmount a gate at Kilmainham Gaol in Dublin, Ireland.

9. The Serpent in Ireland

Ireland is such a watery place, blessed by abundant rain, with water energies that are powerful indeed. Not surprisingly, a plethora of serpent beings are found in animist tradition there. In the era of St Patrick, who supposedly introduced Christianity to Ireland, this had to be purged from society. The pagans (a word meaning rural folk), the peasant population, fiercely opposed destruction of their belief system. Thus it was necessary to create a swag of propaganda, such as that St Patrick supposedly banished Ireland's 'snakes'. There never were any actual snakes in Ireland. But supernatural serpents, worms and eels were ubiquitious in the land, and, worse for the new regime - water and sovereignty goddesses and underworld fertility deities, such as divine duo Aine and Crom Dubh, held sway in the peoples' affections. In effect, Patrick was battling the indigenous paradigms of the day.

No real, live snakes ever lived in Ireland. And a thorough reading of the miraculous adventures of Patrick reveals that he usually only 'banished' them or moved them from one lake to another. Yes, that's right, the serpent spirits are still there!

Certainly I have seen 'serpents eggs' in quiet country backwaters, as in the picture on the left (these being situated above a very early Jesus image!) The round, water washed stones at out-of-the-way healing springs and holy wells were still being used into the twentieth century in ritual fertility practices. To encourage pregnancy, women would take them back to their homes for a while.

Such traditions have survived in rural backwaters because they are more deeply ingrained than the foreign influence of Christianity. It was as a result of a political shift of the day that the Church was able to dominate the people, but the new creed was anathema to their Earth centred spirituality, the traditions of living in harmony with the land, their Mother. The defenders of the pagan faith possibly had a serpent as their emblem. A curious amalgam of belief systems eventually emerged, whereby certain pagan practices were incorporated or tolerated by the Church and allowed to continue on in thinly veiled form.

The Devil's Mother was a name once employed against an Irish goddess, the Caorthannach, who was depicted as a wide-jawed serpentine monster, who could also manifest as a bird or a beautiful woman. A female genius loci of watery places, old Patrick was said to have pursued Her to a springhead at Tullaghan, County Sligo. Tullaghan Hill was once a stronghold of pagan harvest festivals, thus fuelling Patrick's missionary zeal. Patrick was also said to have driven a serpent away from Glen Tachar, in County Donegal, where the serpent Tachar was said to have 'presided over the valley', according to an 1835 account.

Lough Derg, also in Donegal, is the site for one of Ireland's greatest pilgrimage centres. To here, the propaganda goes, the Devils Mother, goddess Corra this time, enticed St Patrick, having assailed him on top of Croagh Patrick, the primary Irish holy mountain, some 152 km away. Michael Dames notes that Lough Derg was previously (in an 1839 guide) called Loch na Corragh and that Corra, the featherless queen of bird demons, is the airborne equivalent of the water serpent Caorthannach. Corr means stork, a mountain peak and also a well or pool in Irish Gaelic.

In the ruddy waters of the lough the goddess Caorthannach lay coiled, in her serpent form, in wait for Patrick. When he approached She swallowed him whole and for two days and nights he tried to cut himself free with his sword. Eventually he got out and was able to kill Her. Her body was turned to stone and the rocks jutting out of the brown waters of the lough are said to be stained with Her blood. Derg means red. Rocks and islands there are also said to Her petrified body, while some believe that She still lies stuck at the bottom of the lough, only arising during storms and *"riding the waves like a wild horse with a flowing mane, froth boiling away at its sides"*.

It was a bit of a case of 'been there, done that already'. Earlier legends attribute a tale of being swallowed by, and then slaying, a serpent to a more ancient hero. The great Irish hero Finn McCool was said to have been a prolific slayer of serpents. Plagiarism was easier to get away with in those days. Modern scholars have found no evidence that Patrick ever went to Lough Derg at all. They say that the historical Patrick was actually a fabrication, his life stories cobbled together from the lives of several male heroes that came before him, Dames reports.

Some accounts say that Patrick banished many serpents, including their chief, the Corra, into a hollow at the north base of the mountain Croagh Patrick itself. Another version of the story says that the 'demon fiend' escaped and took the form of a beautiful woman who went to live with Crom Dubh, the underworld god of the harvest, at his seat at Downpatrick Head (Dun Briste) on the Mayo north coast. She went on to have two children by him, but they were turned into dogs by Patrick. Local legends also allude to Her presence there, saying that old Crom had a fairy mistress who gave him knowledge.

Whatever did happen in the Patrick myth (if any of it!), to this day the Lough Derg pilgrimage is still much celebrated and was first recorded in the 12th century. It really put Ireland on the map and, by medieval times, it was the most well known destination in the country. Seekers taking the cathartic journey within, a vision quest to the underworld, and the return and re-birth at St Patrick's Purgatory, follow a classic tradition in a ritual landscape that continues strongly to this day. (Mere tourists are not welcomed during pilgrimage time!)

It was probably well before St Patrick's time that pilgrims started to go to a cave on Saints Island, said to be previously sacred to Saint Daveog, to undergo their own vision quest and symbolic death and rebirth. (Davach is a related name, meaning vat or large stomach.) The custom was to first fast and pray before entering the dark, cramped cave and to spend twenty four stuffy and uncomfortable hours there. After which pilgrims went stark naked for ritual immersion three times in the cold lake waters, at a spot known as Patrick's Pool.

Beneath St Patrick's Purgatory there was said to be a spring and in 1517 a visitor reported the cave as being called the Well of St Patrick. Probably it was once considered the fertile belly (vat) of the goddess. Wells and springs have long been thought of as entrances to the underworld.

It all got a bit much for the Church, which closed the cave by Papal Decree in 1497. Pilgrims continued on in another cave. Numerous suppression orders followed in the 17th and 18th centuries. But attitudes changed and in 1780 the Station Island cave became a chapel, followed by the building of a huge basilica church dedicated to Mary. These days the island is covered with ecclesiastical buildings.

St Barry's Well, Co. Roscommon

Elsewhere in Ireland, at the other great pilgrimage centre of Glendalough, not far from Dublin, St Kevin also supposedly displaced a serpent from the Upper Lake, and moved it to the Lower Lake, where it *"stopped being a threat to men and beasts"*. In County Kerry St Connla was said to have killed a great serpent that resided at Lisnapeasta in Kilconly parish.

In County Roscommon St Barry battled with Oll Phiast – the Great

Serpent - who lived on a hill, Slieve Badhan, near Strokestown. Barry was said to have chased it towards Lough Lagan, where it plunged in and vanished. The saint had tried to spear the serpent with his crozier and at the spot where his knee touched the ground a well sprung up, which is said to retain his blessing to this day.

St Barry's well remains revered today, a delightful spot with its circular stone enclosure and stately be-ribboned Ash tree. My own dowsing survey of the site found a serpentine energy form projecting upwards there. It's obviously hard to keep a good serpent down!

At Lough Allen (pictured above), the first big lake on Ireland's biggest river, the Shannon, Aillfhion is the resident lake spirit. If feeling aggrieved Aillfhion can strike with vengeance by whipping up a storm in minutes, legends warn. Sudden storms there have had deadly consequences for many people caught out on boats. Reports of sightings of a mysterious creature on the lake give it a large head and *"several undulations of her serpent-like body breaking through the surface of the water"*, says Meehan.

In another legendary sighting, a *"giant worm, eight feet long"* chased and terrorized a milkmaid, in a story collected by Lady Gregory around 100 years ago. And, more recently, serpentine 'horse-eels' in loughs were reported by several eye-witnesses to dragon chaser Ted Holiday.

A 'horse-eel' is the subject of a story Eddie Lenihan collected from an old-timer in south west Ireland in the early 1990's. It was seen by a thatcher who had been cutting reeds on the lake edge all day, as evening was approaching. Suddenly, from out of a corner of a field came a wheel, the size of a penny farthing bicycle wheel, rolling towards the thatcher. As it passed him he saw that it wasn't a wheel but actually an eel, *"about ten feet long"*, rolling along with its tail in its mouth.

The next night he watched it pass again and was close enough to see that it had a *"big, long mane o'hair down along its back, just like a horse."* The third time the man sees the other-worldly eel he kills it, so as to show it to his wife who thought he was inventing a drunken tale. This doesn't turn out to be a very good idea. The next morning he injures his foot badly and from that moment on can never go back to thatching.

But he never earned any sympathy from the neighbours, who, especially the older ones, could have told him he was asking for trouble in killing that being, explaining that: *"That was one o' the people that live in those lakes, carrying a message to some other lake. 'Twas going about its own business, doing no harm to him or anyone else. And he should have done the same, mind his own business. But he didn't. And he paid the price."*

Pan-European Celtic serpent

Many of Irelands legendary serpent beings have heads adorned with ram's horns. This is no doubt a form derived from her continental Celtic heritage. Across Europe, rams-horned serpents can be seen in various artforms, and most famously on the panels of the 2,000 odd year old Gundestrap Cauldron, which boasts three. Here one is typically in association with masculine nature god of the European Celts - Cernunnos, the Horned One. Sporting antlers and surrounded by other animals, Cernnunos is often seen holding or feeding a horned serpent - a depiction of his mastery over the Earth's forces, I imagine.

10. Australian Rainbow Serpents

Across the continent of Australia many species of devas are recognised by Aboriginal people and water snake spirits are common and widespread. One of the most well known and highly revered of these beings is the Rainbow Serpent, who, together with other Dreamtime spirits, was said to have created the landscape features on its mythic journeys across the unformed land at the dawn of the time. In its travels its movements made rivers, gorges and channels in the land.

A dynamic ever-present force in the landscape and giver of the Law, fundamental to spirituality, the Rainbow Serpent represents a primal source of creative inspiration. It could also be classified as the highest level of water deva in the landscape, associated with watercourses, sacred waterholes and waterways, as well as thunderstorms; and responsible for the total balance of water in a region. The term Rainbow Serpent can refer to a major culture hero and landscape creator as well as its lesser, regional manifestations.

A protector of the land and its people, and the source of life giving powers, the Rainbow Serpent can be a destructive force if it is not properly respected. It can inspire awe and fear, and if waterholes are disturbed it can roar with anger, its voice the thunder. Its wrath might raise a waterspout or make a flood.

Sometimes taking the form of rainbow, some kinship groups consider this an unfriendly form and a greatly feared one. In Australia's south, however, the rainbow is not usually associated with water snake spirits.

Coming in many sizes and levels of importance, Rainbow Serpents may be regarded as either being male, female or androgenous. They often

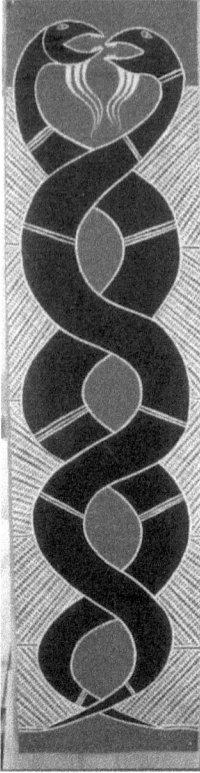

occur in male/female pairs, as in the contemporary painting on the left.

Water Python by Adam Henwood, of the Dreaming of Rex Wilfred of Ngukurr, NT (with permission).

In Northern Australia

Rainbow Serpents first appeared in northern Australian rock art some 10,000 years ago. Over millenia the forms that they took have evolved and diverged. Generally speaking, images of Rainbow Serpents show colourful snake-like or composite beings, often with bizarre appendages. On Tiwi Island is found the more lizard-like Maratji, a huge (up to 90m long), colourful, horned being with long projecting jaws. Around the Top End this creator being is often shown sporting a long mane of hair and a beard. In Groote Eylandt (Gulf of Carpentaria) the great spirit Ipilya lives in a big swamp and is a giant, long haired, whiskered gecko lizard who, each wet season, brings on the monsoon rains.

A study of serpents depicted in west Arnhem Land rock art finds a great majority resembling sea horses and pipefish, with their distinctive tubular snouts and head angles set at 90 degrees. These sea spirits have the brood pouches and prehensile tails of seahorses, as well as some features of yams. (Over the previous 30,000 or so years edible yams, grown as a staple crop and revered in a cult, had dominated artistic expression.) Serpents that resemble Ribboned Pipefish feature long earlike projections and other appendages; they also have a dorsal fin.

It was only in later times that familiar snake-like Rainbow Serpents started to be painted. Other more modern depictions around the Top End show composite beings, such as a kangaroo head with a crocodile tail, or a feathered head with whiskers and waterlillies on its back. Some part water buffalo beings have even been painted, the buffalo being a relatively recently introduced animal. One of these composite Rainbow Serpent beings is seen in a large painting that looks down on travellers from high in the foyer of Darwin Airport.

For the Wardaman tribe around the Katherine area the Rainbow Serpent is personified by a local snake, the Black Headed Python. Originally a landscape creator hero from the Dreamtime, in myth it retired to dwell in the sky and is seen high above the Earth in October, between Scorpius and Crux, its tail bright in the Australian Triangle stars, near where its black nebula head is seen.

Around Tennant Creek the Warramunga people revere Wanambi snake spirits. One such individual, the Wollunqua, lives in the Thapanarlu waterhole in the Murchison Ranges. In its journeys during the creation period of the Dreamtime it stopped at eleven sites to release spirit children. Anthropologists Spencer and Gillen recorded ceremonies at these sites, describing superbly decorated mounds and ground paintings executed to appease Wollunqua.

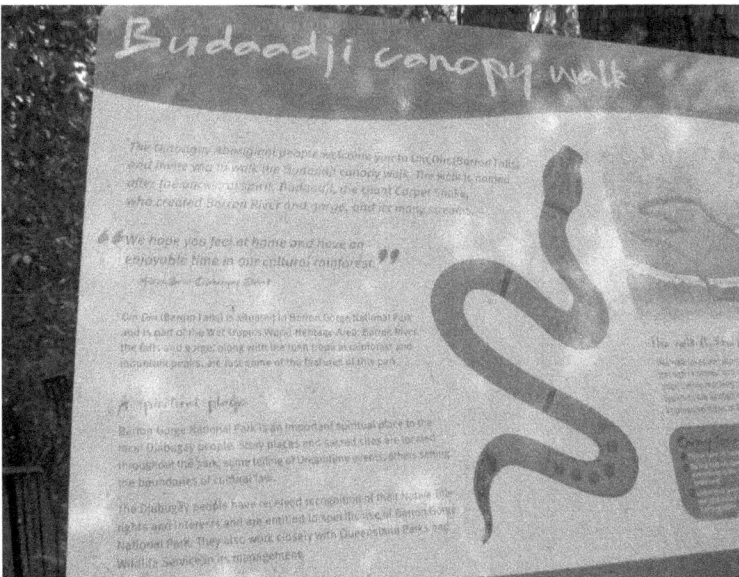

A rainbow serpent in Queensland.

A dangerous Wanambi is said to live in a maze of caverns beneath the steep sided rock hole on the south side of Uluru (Ayers Rock). Anthropologist Mountford was told that it is hundreds of metres long with huge projecting teeth, a beard and opalescent skin. If made angry it has the capability of withdrawing all the sources of water, not just from Uluru, but from around the vicinity. However not all Wanambis are fearsome. At the mesa of Mt Conor, not far away, a friendly Wanambi lives in Aneri Springs.

In Victoria

The great Mindi (Mindye) is a huge and much feared snake spirit, up to several kilometres long and a pre-eminent protector of waterways. Traditionally the terror of the Kulin nation, Mindi does the bidding of Bundjel, the great eagle, a father creator spirit and totemic being. On Bundjel's bidding Mindi metes out punishment for those who break the law. He has a fearsome reputation, though I'm not convinced that he is all bad.

Mindi sports a black mane and a three pronged tongue. He can extend or contract his dimensions when ordered by Bundjel, thus he is able to *"ascend the highest trees and hold on to a branch like a ring tailed possum and stretch his body across a great forest to a great length, so as to reach any tribe,"* Edgar Morrison relates.

Mindi has helpers too, other totemic beings including the Stumpy Tailed Lizard. Mindis manifest here and there in the landscape, as fractal forms, local spirits that dwell at various important Dreaming sites.

When white people invaded Victoria in the 1830s, deadly outbreaks of smallpox swept the land and this decimated the Aboriginals. They called this previously unknown condition the 'scales of Mindi', thinking it must be a punishment sent from Bundjel.

Bark figures fashioned to depict sacred serpents have been recorded from this era. Twenty odd foot long images of Mindi were set up during corroborrees (dance / theatre shows) in an attempt to appease his wrath, reported A. E. Parker, at Australia's first Aboriginal Protectorate, in the district of Franklinford, central Victoria, in 1841. Parker noted that

"It was to appease his anger and avert his destructive influence that was the avowed purpose of the only ceremonies I have ever witnessed bearing any resemblance to an act of worship.... Rude images of the Serpent, consisting of one large and two smaller figures, cut in bark and painted, were set up in a secluded place. ...The men, and afterwards the women, dressed in boughs, and having each a small wand with a tuft of feathers tied in it, were made to dance in single file and in a very sinuous course, toward the spot and after going around it several times to approach the main figure and touch it reverentially with the wand".

West Australian Woggal

In the south west of Western Australia the pre-eminent snake spirit of Noongar (Aboriginal) people is known as the Woggal (or Waugyl or Wahgal). Revered as the guardian of sacred landscapes, it was regarded as a healer, but it could also cause sickness and mete out punishment for broken laws. This powerful snake spirit was invariably described as feathered, finned, maned, or horned, Daisy Bates reported in 1925. It was considered an arbitrator of life and death and *"omniscient and omnipotent amongst the Bibbulmun"*, she said.

Residing in certain springs, pools, hills, caves, gorges and trees the Woggal could be an unfriendly and fearsome guardian spirit. It's stations were winnaitch (taboo) and any game seeking refuge in them was left alone. When passing near the Woggal's home fresh rushes might have been strewn by people, or some cooked meat placed at the foot of a sacred rock or on the edge of Woggal's pool, to propitiate it.

Perhaps the most well known Woggal site is in Perth, on the banks of the Swan River at Goonininup. Local legend tells of a pair of Woggals who presided over the Swan River and surrounds. Goonininup is just below the popular Kings Park water garden on Mount Eliza, at the old

Swan Brewery site. Here gush fresh water springs and thus Goonininup was an important camp ground for the Noongars. It also doubled as a religious site for initiates on their path to adulthood. Goonininup was the place where the Woggal moved between the river and the land. The female laid an egg here that was once visible as a large rock. Despite knowing of its significance, early white settlers removed the egg stone.

After the Brewery closed down the state government pondered on what to do with this top piece of real estate. Noongar protestors camped there from the late 1980's to the early 1990's, trying to stop any more development of the highly sacred site. But developers won in the end and the old brewery has now been transformed into luxury riverside apartments, plus a micro brewery, café and restaurant.

Noongar elder Trevor Walley explained the Woggals significance at a Museum of WA exhibit in Perth thus:

"The Woggal shaped the rivers, waterways and freshwater springs,' wrote 'Woggal controls the rain and weather and ensures there'll always be freshwater. Once Woggal creates the rivers and springs it stays in the features it has formed."

Walley described one Woggal, living in West Australia's Murray River, near the Ravenswood bridge, as being:

"As thick as a tractor tyre, with a snake head and a horses mane and scales the colour of the rainbow... We tell the little kids not to throw rocks at the Woggal, otherwise it will swim around in circles making whirlpools to try to drag you in... (But) if you belong to that country you are safe from accidental drowning and the Rainbow Serpent will save your life".

Elsewhere in the country other similar snake spirits are revered by Aboriginal people, including Kurrea in New South Wales; Moha Moha, the great sea serpent of Queensland's Great Barrier Reef, and many other water beings, in Australia's rich geomythos.

The Rainbow Serpent today

Rainbow Serpents are still out here, guarding and enjoying the waterholes and waterways that are still reasonably intact. Or looking for new homes, where they can exist in peace; for the Earth does not give up its spirit denizens easily, I've found!

The Goonininup Woggal of Perth has moved its home higher up into the artificial waterway in Kings Park, where white people often now come to meditate and attune to nature. A modern sacred site has thus arisen! I sometimes take students there to meet the Woggal, who also seems to get a buzz out of the interaction.

In Australia's central Victoria the snake spirits that my sensitive friends and I have encountered around Maldon are definitely friendly. We often visited and honoured a pair of them at their sacred site home, The Rock of Ages, not from from where we lived. They would also pop over and visit us, exhibiting great curiosity and sometimes wrapping themselves around the Power Tower in the garden, to soak up its vibrant energies.

Divining a stone serpent

I first heard about the 'stone serpent' around the year 2000 and I wondered if I'd ever get to see it myself. This enigmatic stone arrangement had not long before been discovered by local historian John Tully as he explored a remote mountainside in central Victoria. Soon after its discovery, a second and larger, serpentine stone arrangement came to light on another mountain in the region. These are possibly the only two of this kind of monument known today. The site has been officially recorded since then, but no proper archeological study made of it, and local Aboriginal knowledge is fragmented. The local clanspeople used it ceremonially until white man's diseases wiped out many of them by the 1830s, followed by the loss of lands from pastoralism soon after and the 1850's goldrushes - destroying much of their oral culture in the process.

However historical references reveal that the site was once of enormous Dreaming significance, one of a number of serpent spirit sites in the region. John Tully's research leads him to think it could actually be the most significant stone arrangement in all of the state of Victoria.

One mild sunny winter's day John took me and husband Peter Cowman to the site. We drove a very rough track to half way up the mountain slope, then climbed the rest on foot. The forested slopes were dotted with pink granite boulders and winter wildflowers as we headed towards a steep hidden valley where the arrangement began. There were little in the way of tracks where we were going.

But as we got nearer, John pointed out a stone edged section of track that was now taking us towards our destination. We pondered the reason for its existence, but there was no other logical explanation, other than it being an Aboriginal ceremonial track on a steep section.

Following along above the line of the mostly dry creek, we eventually reached a pool of water that seemed to indicate a spring. *"There's always water in that pool,"* John said. A reliable source of water would have been important for a ceremonial centre, where groups of people once spent time together at their cyclic gatherings.

A very large granite boulder lay not far from the pool. *"I reckon this rock is the start of the stone arrangement. I think of it as the head of the serpent,"* said John. (I now think it is more likely the 'tail'.)

Heading away from that big boulder ran a line of smaller, vertically stacked rocks laid in an intermittent path that connected other boulders and rocky ridges together, as it 'slithered' some 180m up the mountainside. Missing sections had been presumably washed away in storms, their rocks scattered below. The most intact sections were tucked away beneath protective bushes and dead trees, which also made them difficult to photograph (as in the photo next page). Judging by the patina and lichen on the carefully arranged remnant rocks, it seemed to be of a venerable age.

Pendulum dowsing the line of stones, I soon detected a sinuous telluric energy flow that followed the path exactly. This energy flow suggested where missing stones had once been placed. One might describe its form as a toroidal vortex flowing horizontally across the surface of the ground. In Ireland, an equivalent energy line might be called a Fairy Path / Fairy Pass. Telluric currents provide popular pathways for nature spirits to move along, as global traditions concur.

After climbing a while we stopped at a level clearing with lovely views. It felt special. (The energy of so much pink granite is pretty awesome, for one!) John pointed out a large boulder that looked very like a Stumpy Tailed Lizard. It had long ago had other stones added to it, as legs, to presumably increase the resemblance. Could this spot have been a special ceremonial site within the greater ritual landscape? A message came to me clairaudiently, that indeed this was the case.

Dowsing on the flattish, clear area beside the Lizard Rock I discovered the vestiges of an upward geo-spiral or Earth vortex, its energy flowing upwards. To me, the vortex would appear to denote a place where people had been dancing in ceremony. I find them in the centre of bora grounds/corroborree sites, across Australia's eastern half. Recently I dowsed a big vortex at an ancient dance site at a regional, biennial Aboriginal dance festival we attended at Laura in far north Queensland. After a weekend with 500 traditional dancers performing fabulously, kicking up a storm of dust, I was impressed by the power of the vortex. Checking the circular site after the dancing had ended, it was still the strongest vortex I'd ever dowsed!

Higher up on Mindi's mountain we followed the lines of arranged stones that connected together sections of granite bedrock in the figure. Intriguingly, there was a part of the line, on a small ridge of bedrock, whose path had been marked for several metres by two small trunks of tough-wooded Lightwood trees (seen below). Although cut by a steel axe, the logs look like they have lain there undisturbed for decades.

Peter Cowman left, John Tully right,
examine the wooden section of the Stone Serpent.

Finally we reached the end at another flattish meadow, with a large granite boulder where the stone arrangement stopped. Previously John had brought my Irish dowser friend here. Sandy Griffin had detected that beneath this snake-head-shaped rock lay a great pool of underground water. This may well be a part of the spring system that feeds the creek below. John Tully had discovered that the pattern of the geology beneath the site was echoed by the path of the stone arrangement. It seemed that the stone serpent was following the water carrying fault lines in the rock, tracking the waters from their origin within the Earth, an underground pool guarded by Mindi, going steeply down the mountainside until arriving at the water's emergence point, the spring in the valley below. I tuned in by dowsing to confirm the abundant water energy around Mindi's sacred head/home.

Yes, Mindi still lives there, guarding that watery site surrounded by a parched, dry landscape. To my vision, he was a sleepy looking Mindi, and as curious about us strangers as we of him. Both he and the site didn't feel at all threatening, just sadly neglected. Mindi appreciated that I use careful protocol before visiting such sites. In advance of our climb I had respectfully asked from a distance if I was welcome to visit him there. In response, he was eager and happy.

Close by the final boulder I soon dowsed a powerful geo-spiral some 10m or so across and more powerful than the previous vortex. The site felt to be of greatest importance, with the most dancing and ceremonial activity occurring there. It remains today a beautiful, wild Dreaming site for communing with the spiritual reality of nature and the supreme local landscape guardian - Mindi, the water spirit.

Mindi's stone head, perhaps?

53

11. Water and sovereignty goddesses

Originally the divinity of water in landscapes and oceans was nearly always equated with the female principle. For over 20,000 years in Old Europe, back in the Paleolithic and Neolithic eras, with its mostly matrifocal, matrilineal cultures, goddesses ruled the divinity of all nature, land and weather. Goddesses governed tribal territory and were often the chief divinity presiding over a watershed or bio-region, with all its waters held particularly sacred to Her.

If not depicted as sacred water snakes, the earliest goddesses were invariably shown as, or with, sacred water birds (cranes, herons, geese and swans) in the art forms that have been left as testimony.

Over in India we find hymns of water goddess worship in the Vedas, earliest of sacred texts and dating from around the middle of the second millennium BCE. A few hymns are dedicated to The Waters, maternal goddesses who purify and nourish. The source of all the gods and universe, these mothers wash away guilt and bring health, wealth and immortality.

The Egyptian word for water *nt* was probably the root word of several names for water spirits, including naiad, nixe and nymph. The Semitic word *mu* and Phoenician/Hebrew *mem* no doubt begat the name of the sea in French, la mer, and also la mere for mother; plus water goddesses such as Mary and Miriam, as well as the sea mother of the Finns and Saami people Mere-Ama. Then there are the Morgan, Celtic sea sprites and Morgan who is also an individual sea goddess in Brittany; while in Ireland Moruadh is the green haired Irish sea maiden and Muireartach, the wild stormy, one-eyed sea goddess there. A mare is a female horse and 'water horses' are common to many global myths.

Not all water spirits are female, or, more technically speaking, of a yin nature. Water's spirits can manifest as yin or yang. Water goddesses often had consorts who ruled with them over various aspects of territory. And sometimes water goddesses were paired up with sun gods, the ultimate yin-yang connection. Such divinely dynamic duos are often associated with hot springs.

While these goddesses have largely faded from the modern mind, legendary fish-tailed mermaids and the like fan the flames of their memory. Ireland's river goddesses are still remembered, as is Cally Berry, the 'water hag' of Northern Ireland, who has equivalents in the south (Cailleach Bhearra) and also in Scotland. This spirit of lakes protects them from being drained, while She also cares for other watercourses in Her territory. Cally is also said to control the weather and when She appears as a crane with sticks in Her beak, She forecasts storms. Being a triple goddess, She can appear in other forms, such as a fish-tailed maiden or motherly figure as well.

The Hag Rock, Bhearra Peninsula, Co. Cork, where I Bhearra may be perceived to be still stationed, looking out for her sea god lover.

Women that shape-shift into crane/heron type water birds feature in some stories in Ireland's ancient annals. Possibly of ancient totemic import, cranes were never eaten as food, although it's highly possible they were sacrificed in some sort of Celtic crane cult. A sorceror's stance when casting magic spells, pronouncing maledictions and satirical verse, was to stand on one leg with one arm raised and one eye closed, perhaps in imitation of this bird's hunting pose. An old woman, in Ireland's Da Derga's Hostel legend, cursed a king who refused her entry using this very stance. (Likewise the god Lugh was said to have blessed the soldiers of his army with strength and courage *"on one foot and with one eye"*.)

This pose is also seen in three of the one hundred or so remaining Sheela-na-gig carvings in Ireland. These stone figures of raunchy or frightening females are mainly from the Medieval era. Sheelas appear to have had a protective function and were talismans of female power, displaying the goddess's hag/wisdom aspect, in often startlingly exhibitionist poses.

Sheela na Gig at Stepaside, Co. Dublin, unique in its original location beside a well.

Female deities were largely usurped with the Indo-European invasions of patriarchal tribes that swept in from the Russian steppes. A melange of the two spiritual polarities thus developed after 2,500 BC and the classic cosmologies, in which gods raped the goddesses, record those changing times in later, blended traditions.

Images of Celto-Roman mother goddesses have been found at sacred wells across Europe. In a carving at Coventina's well on Hadrian's Wall in England The Matres (Mothers), as the triple

Coventina, are seen seated, holding a water jug in one hand and pouring out a stream of water from the other. Three goddesses are also depicted on a plaque discovered in the ancient Roman bathing complex at Bath. (They may well be representing the triple nature of a single goddess, as maiden, mother and crone.)

An Irish Mary figure stands on top of a serpent.

Queen of the South Seas

In the Indo-Pacific region, water deities are often sea-going. In Yogyakarta, a cultural capital of Indonesia, ancient animist traditions make this city beholdent to a regal sea deity who carries the titles of Loro Kidul (Queen of the South Seas), Kanjeng Ratu Kidul (Supreme Southern Queen) and Roro Kidul (The Southern Maiden).

Manifesting as a beautiful goddess dressed in green, She controls the nearby sea and sea bed on the southern coast of Java. She is also the traditional protector of the once-powerful Mataram Dynasty and its current descendants, the sultans of Yogyakarta. The Queen is married spiritually to those descendants.

She is said to live under the ocean at Parangtritis, a beautiful black-sand beach village about 30 km south of Yogya's city centre. When angered she can whip up tsumanis and sieismic mayhem, so the local people regularly appease Her with offerings to invite Her goodwill.

The Queen's waterfront shrine at Parangkusumo beach is close to where an original legendary meeting of the goddess and the local sultan once occurred, on two flat-topped pieces of volcanic rock. Here also is where the annual ceremony of Labuhan is performed.

Each year, on the 30th day of the Javanese month of Rejeb, offerings are given to the goddess. These consist of food and clothing, plus all of the Sultan's hair and fingernail cuttings from the previous year. The offerings are cast into the sea in the hope that the Sultan and the people of Yogyakarta enjoy continuous peace and prosperity.

In troubled times, sultans of Yogyakarta made their way through an underground network of caves to Parangtritis to seek out the Queen's advice. This last happened in the final days of Suharto's reign in early 1998, when the city's current leader made the journey, The Australian newspaper reported. The next day a million people gathered outside the palace and the sultan suggested to them that Suharto should step down, which he duly did, the next day.

Balinese water goddess

On the fabulous volcanic island of Bali, also in Indonesia, an intricate sharing system provides irrigation water for the fertile rice paddies upon which the island depends. To be successful, rice growing requires careful timing of planting, crop rotation and the efficient and timely use of large quantities of water.

The Balinese revere the island's waters as a divine gift from their water goddess Dewi Danu, who oversees the complex management of an elaborate network of irrigation channels administered from temples controlled by priests. Bali has many famous water temples that are located beside its lakes, irrigation canals and reservoirs. The priests of these temples are the managers of the water and arbitrators of water disputes.

Pura Ulun Danu Bratan (pictured next page) in Bedugul is the most

important and well known of these water temples. It presides over a picturesque volcanic crater lake nearly one mile (1.6 km) above sea level, where the air is much cooler and lush pine forests thrive. This temple, consecrated in 1663, is the seat of Dewi Danu and here She is attended by Her 24 priests. The high priest, Her human representation, holding the title Jero Gde, was chosen in childhood by the goddess to serve until his death.

The temple controls about half of Bali's agricultural land, managing a highly productive system that involves an intricate complex of canals, weirs, tunnels and ditches connected to 74 square miles of paddy fields. Festivals take place here as well, and the temple functions as an important social hub.

The Balinese have relied on their ritual-based system of irrigation for at least 1,000 years. The temples are strategically placed at each level or diversion of the irrigation path. Every field has a temple in a corner too and here farmers show their gratitude for the rice crop with prayers and offerings given.

Paddy fields are organized into co-ops called subaks. Subak leaders ascend to the temple where prayers, offerings and meetings take place.

These are to ensure a good crop for all and for subaks far downstream to have enough water to sustain their paddies.

With their age-old traditions of crop rotation patterns, Bali's rice farmers experience few problems with pests. All is controlled by the beneficent Goddess of the Lake.

When I visited this beautiful lake in April 2008 I was able to clairvoyantly glimpse this powerful goddess. It was a most memorable encounter. We paddled out across the lake at dawn to view the temple and stopped when close to Her presence. After some meditation I offered Her a gift of a special energy ball, which She gladly accepted.

The magnificent goddess reciprocated. I clairvoyantly watched as a squadron of water nymph attendants appeared around us, encircling our canoe, bearing etheric gifts of water lilly blossoms that they surrounded us with. The blossoms persisted in my aura for some days afterwards and I felt well and truly blessed!

12. Sun deities and hot springs

There was once a widespread belief, fairly universal, that the Sun travels through the underworld at night, refreshing itself in the underground waters there. People would seek healing at such sacred springs by sleeping for a night beside them, perhaps expecting to gain the benefit of the nourishing powers of the underground Sun. (This helps to explain why hot springs were so highly venerated.)

The Wardaman tribe of northern Australia also have a similar tradition. They say the Sun sinks at dusk under the ground and goes into the subterranean waters there, which the Rainbow occasionally releases to the surface as springs. Wardaman describe the Sun as going down through a big tunnel into the watery underworld, through a canopy of weeds that protect the underground waters and retain the Sun's warmth. The Sun returns to the surface each day in the east at dawn, all cleansed and refreshed. A spring is the 'eyeball of the Rainbow', the Wardaman say.

On the other side of the world, at a French shrine at Mont Dol near St Malo, morning ceremonies at four sacred springs once celebrated the Sun's daily emergence from the underworld. In Burgundy a major solar water shrine had a sanctuary in the shape of a sun wheel. Situated beside the River Cure at Les Fontines Salees, this shrine was later developed and expanded by the Romans.

Irish landscape goddesses Aine and Grian are also sun deities. They are possibly sister goddesses, Grian being the weak winter sun and Aine the bright summer sun. Aine means bright or glowing and She is also known as Anu and Danu in Kerry and elsewhere in the south-west. Danu was chief goddess, and mother of all gods, for the Tuatha da Danann tribe, whose arrival probably heralded the beginning of the Bronze Age in Ireland. This tribe was adept at working gold and bronze, much of which was emblazened with sun motifs.

The Paps of Anu, two breast shaped hills in County Cork, were once considered emblematic as fonts of the goddess's goodness. The beginning of the harvest festival, around August 1st, used to be held there. In Christian times it became a berry-picking festival held on St Latiaran's Sunday, the last Sunday in July. A nearby well, named after the goddess Red Claws (Crobh Dearg's Castle), is where cattle were once herded to the water annually at May Eve, in an ancient ritual to ward off disease for the coming year. Such rituals of cleansing and protection, with animals driven through water, were once a common practice in Ireland.

At Cullen, not far from the Paps, is St Latiaran's well, with its attendant sacred white thorn tree and famous Curtsey Stone, a heart shaped boulder honoured by women on the harvest festival day. Latiaran had two sisters, these being Lassair ('flame') and Inghean Bhuidhe, the 'yellow-haired daughter'. Older traditions of three sacred women, of Anu, Babdha and Macha; and also Latiaran, Crobh Dearg and Gobnai, reveal their goddess origins. When these three firey females disappeared from Earthly existence they left three sacred wells behind them, at Cullen, Cahercrovdarrig and Ballyvourney, legend goes.

Bridgid was another sun and landscape goddess and in Christian times St Bridget took over Her role. Bridget's name means 'bright arrow'. St Patrick replaced sun god Lugh as a symbol of light and many sacred springs were re-dedicated to Sts Patrick and Brigit, in an attempt to Christianise the annual pilgrimages to them.

At Her shrine at Kildare, Bridgid /St Bridget had a temple with a perpetual fire burning, representing her passionate flame of knowledge. It was tended by nineteen virgin priestesses and located near a sacred well. (This is similar to how other fire goddesses were worshipped – Hestia in Greece and Vesta in Rome, with Her Vestal virgins, in perpetual flame shrines.)

Finally removed for being too pagan during the Reformation, the ancient fire temple tradition was resumed in Kildare in 1993 and continues to this day with the Bridgidine Sisters presiding.

In northern Europe there are many Helen's Wells and these are associated with the goddess Mother Hel/Dame Holle, who gave Her name to holy and healing. Frau Holle, who was ubiquitous in the German-speaking world, was a white woman who bathed at noon in fountains, from where spirits of children then emanated. (Australian Aboriginal lore also says that often the spirits of children are derived from sacred water holes.)

Dame Holle lived in mountain caves or wells and could be visited by diving into the waters. Sunshine was said to stream from Her hair when it was combed and rain would fall when she threw out washing water. She brought gifts of bounty and new technologies to the people, such as the invention of flax spinning. Her feast day is the winter solstice, heralding the lighter half of the year.

In Germany one of the most important sacred sites is at Aachen. Here the imperial cathedral is located over the sacred healing well of Aquae Granni, dedicated to sun god Grannos, who was equated with Apollo.

Worship of the sun came to be demonised as Christianity battled to obtain supremacy. The sacred number of the sun, 666, became transformed into a symbol of the Devil in the Bible. The firey sun goddesses of ancient Ireland became, in later superstition, denigrated as dangerous red-headed women, witchy troublemakers. (Such as the fearsome Red Woman who turned into a 'water-worm' and coiled around her opponents, in an adventure of Finn and his Fianna/band.)

Hot springs

Hot springs were a favourite resting stop of the mythical night sun,
which was thought by Celtic peoples to empower their healing waters.
In Italy, Burmanus/Borvo was a deity of turbulent and hot waters,
accompanied by Burmana/Damona, his female equivalent. Burmanus
has been depicted in a ceramic image with a horned serpent and a
dolphin. He is also associated with a large sacred forest, the Lucas
Burmani, around Cervo in Liguria.

Hot mud pool, Rotorua, New Zealand.

The geothermal spring waters at Bath in south-west England were presided over by local sun/water goddess Sulis and probably her male counterpart, a Grannos/Apollo type snake-haired (Gorgon type) figure whose sunny face is carved in stone there. Bath's goddess is depicted in a life-sized gilded bronze head, which is all that remains there of Her cult statue. The composite title Sulis Minerva reflects on the spiritual hybridisation that occurred in Roman times. Native goddess Sulis's name suggests a sun goddess combined with or evolved from an indigenous well nymph.

The Romans recognised her as Minerva - a goddess with several layers of guise, who seems to have had some of Greek Athena's warlike aspects tacked onto her original attributes. But originally, Minerva was revered as an intellectual, *"wisdom incarnate in female form"* and an inventor of music.

The Romans also referred to Sulis as Minerva Medica, or Healing Minerva, reminding us how colonial concepts are often grafted onto more indigenous traditions (and vice versa) and their divinities recycled, repackaged and re-invented with fresh vigour down through the ages.

Gorgon, British Museum

65

13. Sacred rivers and their deities

Rivers used to be considered sacred from their source to the end and waterfalls were particularly revered. People would sit under waterfalls, as well as practice ritual immersion in pools, in their quest for purification, vitalisation and the renewal of health and spiritual wellbeing. The clergy of Ireland's early Celtic Christian Church continued this tradition and there are stories of some of them meditating as they stood motionless in rivers and holy wells.

Subject to veneration since earliest times across Europe, valuable votive offerings used to be deposited in the sacred rivers, at their sources in particular, to ensure health and prosperity for all (as well as in sacred lakes, pools and bogs). This is evidenced by the numerous and sometimes magnificent artifacts that have been dredged up from underwater sediments. Items of weaponry and armour, as well as skulls and stone heads, were once ritually cast into the sacred waters.

Displays at the London Museum reveal an unbroken practice of offerings thrown into the Thames River from ancient times, starting with Stone Age tools, axes and blades and ending in Roman times with often

The Battersea Shield, an Iron Age votive offering found in the River Thames (London Museum).

66

very valuable and sophisticated weaponry and other items. Swords and lakes also have mystical connections in medieval Arthurian legends, where the Lady in the Lake is the chief water spirit - a wise, beautiful and powerful deva of place.

A belief in the holiness of rivers is evident elsewhere in Britain, with six rivers bearing a name based on Dee, the word derived from deva. Resident river deities, usually female, were the rulers of entire landscape drainage systems, queens of their watersheds. As well as being promoters of the fertility of their bio-region (water catchment area), river goddesses were associated with healing, inspiration and prophecy.

Around the regions of Ireland goddesses of river systems were highly revered. Goddess Boinn inhabits Her sacred river, the Boyne; while the famous megalithic mound of Newgrange beside it perhaps represents Her womb and a (re-)birth canal for the nobles interred there. Celtic European goddess Brigit is remembered in Ireland's River Brigit, in Wales with the Braint and with the Brent River in England. Rivers named Donn also commemorate goddesses, as do several Avon Rivers, sacred to goddess Abnoba. Belisama, another goddess whose name means 'bright one', presides over England's Mersey, Sabrina lives in the Severn and Coventina the Carrawburgh. In Scotland Clota rules over the Clyde, while in France Sequana is goddess of the Seine.

The River Shannon, Ireland.

In Irish legend, River Shannon is ruled by goddess Sionnan / Shannon, grand daughter of Manannan Mac Lir, god of the sea. At a shady pool called the Shannon Pot, in Co. Cavan, in a tale of female denigration and subsequent deification, the mortal Shannon went to partake of the 'forbidden fruit' of knowledge, the sacred salmon, giver of wisdom. But she paid a high price, for the enraged fish lashed its tail, the waters sprang up and overwhelmed her, its flow becoming the sacred river.

Shannon was thus transformed into an immortal river goddess and in the waters of that mighty river here Her spirit remains, I have been able to detect by dowsing. Likewise for Boinn (pronounced Bo-een) in another tale of human sacrifice. She was the wife of water god Neachtain, who, with his brothers, was the keeper of the magical, but forbidden, Well of Segais. This now named Trinity Well is the traditional source of the Boyne River at Carbery, in County Kildare. Carbery used to be called Sidh Neachtain, the fairy mound of Neachtain.

Around this sacred well nine legendary magic hazelnut trees dropped their nuts of knowledge into the waters, to feed the salmon, the wisest being of all. But the well's treasure was well guarded and when Boinn tasted its waters they, too, rose up in fury, pouring out a mighty flood and drowning her, while creating the River Boyne. It was said that anyone drinking from this well in June would become a poet.

These identical themes seem to speak of a lost status of the river goddess and may well reflect changing paradigms, with the arrival of patriarchal warrior tribes around the time of the Iron Age.

Sacred Indian rivers

Over in India, seven rivers enjoy the greatest sanctity and their ruling goddesses are the pre-eminent Ganga, Yamuna and Sarasvati. Sarasvati was the prototypical river devi of the Sarasvati River in north-western India, which has now vanished underground following a seismic disturbance. The Sarasvati was a river said to flow down from the celestial ocean, bringing multiple blessings with it and filtering through Shiva's dreadlocks as He sat meditating on the sacred Mount Kailash, His hair dividing the waters into seven different streams that flowed down into the Earth.

Goddess Ganga is celebrated at the confluence of three rivers at Allahabad, where a huge annual pilgrimage takes place. Later hymns identify Sarasvati with the goddess Vag, the goddess of speech. Vag created the universe and brought language and poetic vision. She is called the 'mother who gives birth by naming things' (a role seen in many other creator deities the world over). Sarasvati also took on such attributes over time and is now associated with learning, poetry, music and culture.

Indian mermaid water goddess (British Museum)

Sacred Nigerian rivers

In Nigeria, Oshun is the pre-eminent river Goddess of fertility and healing for the Yoruba tribe. Her husband is Shango. Oshun is the 'owner of the sweet waters', the goddess of love, sexuality, beauty, pleasure, happiness and diplomacy. She is also responsible for fertility, love and divination. Although She is a great giver, when angry it can be very difficult to calm Her down. During the times of slavery Her cult spread to Middle and South America.

European sirens and nixes

14. European sirens
and nixes

Europe has a great variety of local water beings, from sirens and mermaids to seal-people and water-horses. Merpeople (mermaids and mermen), the most well known, are often described as femme fatales in worldwide legends. Lesser known are the Silkies (also called selkies, selchies, roane and seal-people). These are shape-shifting beings that can change from seal to human form, by removing their sealskins. Stories about Silkies are known from Cornwall, Ireland (especially Co. Donegal) and Scotland (the west coast and northern islands especially).

Female Silkies have long dark hair, mournful brown eyes and enchanting voices. Many a young fisherman in legend has found them irresistible and there are tales of them stealing a Silky's skin to force one to marry them. There is a famous Scottish song on the subject. Silky wives can never forget the sea and when they find their skins they always go back to it, leaving their husbands bereft.

70

Other 'water ladies', or nymphs, have traditionally been regarded as the guardians of springs, wells, fountains, pools and wetlands. Important ones have been called nymph queens. While the 'male' water spirits are often associated with wilder (yang) waters.

Charming little water spirits in the English countryside were reported in the early twentieth century by clairvoyants Bishop Leadbeater and Geoffrey Hodson, with some fascinating descriptions. These Nixes, as they are sometimes referred to, can appear as tiny human-like beings.

Clairvoyant observations of Nixes on river banks, where they love to spend their time absorbing the radiant water energy, especially at water falls, are particularly fascinating.

Their energetic forms are said to delight in absorbing the water energy and inflate greatly in size. They then discharge the energy in a joyful flash, after which, deflated, they relax again, before going through the energising cycle again and again.

The role of the Nixes, says Marko Pogacnik, is to distribute life-sustaining qualities of water throughout the landscape and this they achieve through *"resonance triggered by dance-like movements."*

Not-so-friendly nixes

Not all the legendary water spirits were considered to be entirely benelovent. Sometimes water nymphs were 'femme fatales', especially those whose river got a bit wild at times, especially in mountainous areas. There is a also a long lost tradition of Cursing Wells that were once used for magical work.

River Nixes of Germany were siren-like beings, sometimes in diminutive human form, sporting long blonde hair. Essentially peaceful, they loved to dance and would often enchant a mortal man. At other times ferocious, like their river habitats, they would drown the odd careless person. River Rhine hosted such a spirit, the terrible Lorelle.

Likewise the spirit of the River Ribble near Clitheroe, Lancashire. Beside a well in the grounds of Waddow Hall near Brungerley Bridge is a headless statue once said to represent St Margaret, but now considered to be Peg O'Neill. This dangerous water spirit has been said to claim a life every seven years, although her wrath could be averted by an animal sacrifice. Before the bridge was built there people had to cross the river on stepping stones. After heavy rain upstream the Ribble swells rapidly, making it a treacherous fording spot and the headless statue and legend provided a warning to be extra careful.

In other traditions a river must claim its toll of human victims every year. The annual sacrifice, a widespread archetypal theme in much global mythos, crops up in the Welsh legend of a voice that is heard annually from rivers or lakes, crying: *"The hour is come, but the man is not."* Often dredged up from amongst ancient votive offerings to rivers, human skulls and bones are presumably those of sacrificial victims.

Marvellous mermaids of Melbourne, Australia.

72

15. Water horses

The sacred horse and horse deities

In the mythic tapestry of old European culture, the deity of the sacred horse, as a totemic associate of mankind, has long been connected with water. The horse in battle also enabled nimble warfare and thus horse deities are often associated with war and death.

Water horse in Whitehall, London

Gallic horse goddess Epona also promoted life, being more of a fertility Goddess who ruled over territory. Her cult grew so popular that Her worship spread to Rome, becoming popular amongst Rome's soldiers (when Rome was normally an exporter of beliefs). Epona, like the Matres, is sometimes connected with sacred waters. The Gauls had Epona enshrined near thermal springs, where she is depicted as a naked water nymph, in places such as Allerey and Saulon-la-Chapelle.

Welsh goddess Rhiannon rides a white horse and across Ireland local sovereignty goddesses also ride white horses. Edain Echraidhe is the White Mare Horse Goddess of the Gabhra, a sacred valley between the hills of Tara and Skryne, Co. Meath. She was celebrated at the summer solstice, reports Irish Druid Con Connor. Manannan Mac Lir is the Irish sea god who rides his waters on white maned horses - the frothy waves.

From India to Europe there are traditions of horses being sacrificed to water deities. They are also associated with ceremonies of sacred kingship and allegiance to the land.

In northern Ireland, Macha, sovereignty goddess of Ulster is the horsey war goddess equivalent of Epona. Her great Iron Age palace is at the royal hill site of Emhain Macha, in County Armagh. In 1798 workers found four bronze ceremonial horns, in a Bronze Age lake offering from nearby Loughnashade, the Lake of the Treasures. The only remaining horn, some 6 ft in length, is now in Dublin's National Museum. Its drone can be heard several kilometres away. Another sacred pool not far from Emhain Macha yielded ritual deposits of pottery, worked bone, a human skull and deer antlers – offerings to sovereignty goddess Macha, perhaps. Ulster also has the lake of the horse-riding warrior god Eochaid - Lough Neagh (pronounced just like a horse's 'nay').

The horse totem is also associated with solar deities, who were driven across the sky by horses; thus discs and sun-wheels are often seen depicted with horses as well. Ireland's Macha, Aine, Grianne and others are connected both to the sun and to horses. St Bridget is sometimes represented by a shoe. Perhaps for the earlier goddess Bridgid it was a horseshoe.

Brighid was a patron of blacksmithery as well as poetry, fertility and healing. The blacksmith was once considered a sacred magician, the skillful worker of fire, metal and water in the alchemical act of transformation. Certainly the upturned horseshoe became a symbol of good luck. And just as sacred springs are today's wishing wells, seeing a white horse is still considered lucky.

The Horse Goddess remains never far away, I discovered as I was researching this section. I had my own couple of surprise encounters with white ponies.

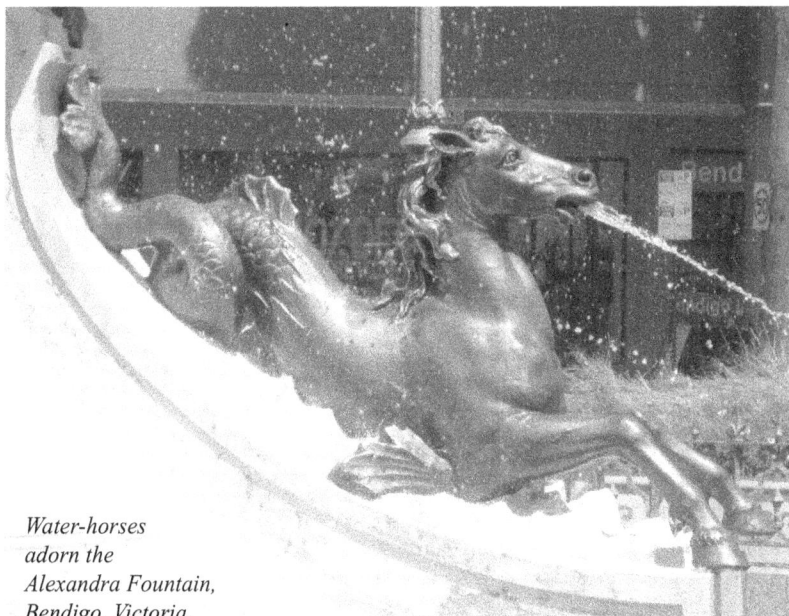

*Water-horses
adorn the
Alexandra Fountain,
Bendigo, Victoria.*

Each Uisge and water kelpies

Lesser water spirits with horsey associations are also widespread in Europe. Water-horses are known from the Scottish Highlands (as Each Uisge), to western Ireland and Scandinavia. With their large seal-like bodies and horse-like heads, dark and dripping wet mane, long eel-like tails, stumpy legs, webbed feet, bright eyes and slimy coat, these creatures can be found lurking wherever there are deep lakes to inhabit.

In Australia Kelpies are normally thought of as a breed of farm dog. In Scotland and Ireland Kelpies are something else - a small species of water-horse whose favourite hunting ground is running water. Feared, they can kill people, by shape shifting to seductive women, or enticing children to ride them, then drowning them; although the males are also known to seduce mortal women. Sometimes they warn of impending storms. And yes, the first individual of that dog breed was named after them.

A malicious hybrid 'man-horse' found in Orkney is known as the Noggely or Nuggle. Although the Nuggle was said to be able to disguise itself as any creature, it usually took the form of a placid but magnificent horse or pony. In Iceland the Nuggle is also found and here it is referred to as a Vatnhestr (meaning water-horse) or Nykur.

The water-horse of wild western Irish loughs intrigued journalist F.W. Holiday, who tried to track it down in the watery corners of Connemara, County Mayo. Here it used to be called the Pieste or Piast, or Payshtha More, the Great Pest. But water-horse, horse-eel or eel-horse were the common names that Holiday mainly heard in the 1960s.

In medieval manuscripts a water spirit called The Great Worm of Hell had Lough Mask as one of its haunts. Mask is a Swedish word for worm. The dragon carved on the O'Flaherty tomb in nearby Oughterard church commemorates an encounter with it at Lough Mask.

Eye witness accounts of several Piests had a general similarity in their descriptions, Holiday said. They were usually greyish black, with a long neck and a horse-like front that tapered off into a long eel-like tail. Some people reported two horn-like projections on their heads, as well.

Often just humps had been seen rising from the water, either two, three or four at a time; while sometimes a big mane was seen around the head, with large shining eyes. Traditions told of how the mystery beings in the lakes would travel overland to other lakes. This helps explain how such big creatures, described as between 10 and 30 ft long, could survive in such small water bodies.

In England Holiday studied dragons in old religious art and found them frequently depicted along similar lines as the descriptions of the water-horses. They are usually shown horned, often having wing-like fins, a seal-like head on a long neck, stumpy leg-like appendages and a rear end tapering off like an eel. One such carving, from the late 7th century, has Jesus trampling a couple of such dragons underfoot, with the horns on their heads plainly visible. Others of similar vintage show a pair of dragons *"worshipping Jesus"*, says Holiday.

16. Lake beings of the world

In Scotland that most classic of water beasties, the 'Loch Ness Monster', has been subject to speculation for centuries. Is it real flesh and blood? A remnant dinosaur? Or is Nessie only imaginary, an hallucination.... or a water spirit? Perhaps all of the above!

Nessie's legendary attributes, according to eye-witness descriptions, have cast it as a dragon or water-horse type being. Similar such creatures lurk in other Scottish lochs. Holiday reports that the Highlanders *"have been calling the dragons of Loch Ness and Loch Morar 'The Great Beast' for many centuries."* Like other Scottish lochs, these lakes are often very deep and enigmatic.

Most investigation into the mystery has flatly failed. The beings appear to have an uncanny ability to show up just when cameras are not around, or when camera film has become jammed. But sonically, large inexplicable things have been detected moving around in Loch Ness. The trouble is, the things are so fast moving that people can't move in close fast enough. The sonic blips disappear into the depths in a flash.

The 'Beasts' have been both celebrated and feared since ancient times, if certain Scottish earthworks are anything to go by. An 1871 report to the British Association speaks of the presence of 'serpent mounds' of earth and stone, with an example being at the lower end of Loch Nell near Oban - a 300 ft long earthwork with a head formed by a stone cairn.

The most dramatic earthwork effigy, however, is on a ridge of Ben Cruachan and is partly formed by three peaks, which become its humps, with a stone cairn for a head. The effigy overlooks Loch Awe and is above the Pass of Brander, noted John S Phene (in 'Reptile Tumuli', Pall Mall Gazette, 1871), Holiday informs us. The 'Great Beast of Loch Awe' was well known in those times.

Back in early Christian times the Church was keen to get rid of the veneration of local water spirits and a Kelpie is recorded as being banished by St Columba from the River Ness, which later became associated with the Loch Ness Monster.

In the 1970's scientists conducting a sonar and photographic survey of Loch Ness, using submarines and automatic cameras, had significant findings and the best evidence yet. In the late 1990's a large hole or cave was reported to have been sonically detected at the bottom of the deep loch. Nessie's lair, perhaps?

Some witness's comments allude to the possibility of either great intelligence and/or telepathic ability of the creatures, and also a certain playfulness in their activities.

Loch Lochy has it's own large water beastie, known as Lizzie. In 1996 newspapers reported that: "...thirty six years after she was last spotted in Loch Lochy, eye-witnesses were stunned to see the 12 ft long, three-humped creature rearing out of the water." (The Scottish Daily Record & Sunday Mail of 15th September 1996).

Sweden also has a famous lake monster, the Storsjoodjuret or Monster of Lake Storsjon, in Jamtland, about 600 km (370 mls) northwest of Stockholm. In July 1996 the creature hit the headlines when a video recording of it was made by a visitor. The creature had humps and was estimated to be 33 to 39 ft long. Recorded sightings date back to 1635, the Ostersund Museum having collected some 500 accounts.

Most sightings there occur in the tourist season, with two or three reported each summer. Folklore says that the lake beings are seasonal and migrate from the Gulf of Bothnia, where they spend the winter. In summer they have been observed on land, moving between the various lakes.

In 1986, after 22 years of sporadic debate, it was declared that anyone trying to capture or kill the Storsjon 'monster' could be prosecuted, while they were *"awaiting a determination of its species"*. This determination never came.

Descriptions of the monster have changed over the years. Nearly all the 19th century witnesses describe a water-horse, its head sporting a long white mane that floats in the water. From the museum's archives, plus interviews with modern eye-witnesses, the typical creature observed is 10 to 16 ft long and 12 to 16 in wide, is dark grey or black and has a relatively small head, reported Fortean Times editor, Paul Sieveking, (The Telegraph, 13/10/96). Dragons, serpents, worms and water-horses seem to be fairly interchangeable forms, it seems.

But it hasn't just been 'lunatics' or tourism promoters that have a firm belief in the existence of real live creatures in the lochs. In British government documents, recently released by Freedom of Information legislation, it turns out that Swedish officials approached the British Foreign Office for advice on how to protect their own Storsjo Monster, as the Thatcher government was determined to protect any rare wildlife, including Nessies, by law. As a result, the Swedish law was passed in 1986. But this protection was overturned in 2005, after arguing over the lack of identification.

Russia may have its own Nessies, with a sighting reported in the Tver region, 80 km (50 mls) northwest of Moscow in Lake Brosno, Itar-Tass news agency reported on 10/12/96. Lake Brosno is about 10 km (six mls) long and 40 m (130 ft) deep. The creature seen and photographed there was about 5 m (16 ft) long. Local newspapers have been reporting sightings of a strange beast in the lake since the 1850s, Tass said.

South Africa may also have a Nessie. Zulu legend in Kwa Zulu-Natal has it *"lurking at the bottom of the 300 ft Howick Falls...exerting a magical force as it sucks victims into its underwater lair... fuzzy photographs show a skinny long neck rising out of a swollen body"*, the Guardian (UK) reported of 'Nessie's Rival' on 13/6/96.

From China are reports of possible water-horses, with sightings of a blond-headed creature at Lake Tianchi (Heavenly Lake) in northeast China's Jilin province. The official news agency said that Eyewitnesses had seen: *"a creature, moving as fast as a walking man, twice in the past two weeks. The swimming creature's blond head surfaced as it swam from north to southwest in the lake for ten minutes, stirring up waves 2 m (7 ft) high, before it submerged"*, said an eye-witness. It was just another one of many sightings and pictures taken of the mysterious creature in modern times, reported The Guardian (UK), on 9/9/94.

Beings of similar description haunt five lakes in Utah, USA, one of which is known as the Bear Lake Monster. Local indigenous people call these beings 'water-babies' and warn that they can catch and eat people, a Utah website warns.

Old Nessie just keeps on popping up!

17. Australasian water beings

Ancient Plesiosaurus?

Australia has had its own modern-day sightings of creatures whose descriptions match closely that of the water-horse of Europe. Just north of Sydney my sister saw what has been called the Broken Bay Monster. While out on a leisurely boating trip she, and others, were amazed to watch a big head on a long neck rear up out of the Bay waters. Although the sighting could be given other explanations, it is not without precedence.

Where it occurred, in the Hawkesbury district, there are large areas of soft sandstone that was perfect for Aboriginal people to carve pictures into. There are vast numbers of petroglyphs, often of game animals and with a history spanning tens of thousands of years. I made several expeditions to view these in the 1980's, taken by John Lough, who has recorded thousands of carvings since he was employed to map them for the highways department, before the massive freeways were built through the Hawkesbury region. (The freeways were then routed to avoid damaging the important carvings.)

Several of those thousands of petroglyphs show an enigmatic large blob a couple of metres or so wide with a long tail / neck extending from it. This could possibly represent a plesiosaurus, an ancient creature presumed extinct. Such carvings are from inland of the same Bay where my sister had her sighting. Although close to Sydney, the Kuringai National Park itself is a vast and rugged wilderness area and this has helped protect the old rock carvings. The petroglyphs are fading fast from erosion and from not being 'refreshed' at intervals. Fortunately John Lough has recorded a great many.

The waters around this wilderness on the fringe of Australia's biggest city are filled with pleasure boats, so it turns out that the Broken Bay Monster has had quite a few sightings since the European invasion. Witnesses around the Hawkesbury River, which flows into the Bay, have described seeing a creature that is greyish-black in colour, with a big bulky body ranging from 7 m to 24 m in length, two sets of flippers, a long neck and serpent-like head, and an eel-like tail.

In a local newspaper report of 1979 we are told of a famous sighting in the Bay, just after World War II, when a Mr Doug Bradbury and another man were out fishing in a small rowboat. It was the reported that:

"Suddenly a giant snake-like head on the end of a long neck, rose six metres above the water. The men dropped their fishing equipment and rowed quickly for the nearby shore. From the shore they were able to get a good look at the creature. It displayed, apart from the long neck and serpent-like head, a large body, with two sets of long flippers which were partly obscured by the water, and a long thick eel-like tail".

The story, archived by the Hawkesbury Historical Society, also told of how, in April 1979, *"a woman watched with binoculars while a 25 m long humped plesiosaur-shaped creature glided slowly under the Hawkesbury River Bridge. A serpent-like head rose above the water on the end of a long neck at least 1.5 m out of the water for a brief 30 seconds before the creature submerged."*

To have seen such a creature so close to a big city seems extraordinary enough and this to be still a mystery in the 21st century is even more amazing. But then again, in another wilderness park near Sydney a brand new species (and genus) of giant conifer tree, the Wollemi Pine, lay hidden in an inaccessible valley, until its discovery just a few years ago.

Author Rex Gilroy has written about these mysterious water creatures and the numerous sightings reported from around Australia's coastline, as well as from New Guinea, New Zealand and elsewhere. The descriptions all have much similarity. The closest real life animal that fits them is the Plesiosaur, an aquatic dinosaur that supposedly became extinct some 70 million years ago. Many fossilised remains have been found in central Australia, once an inland sea, and there is a marvellous opalised skeleton of one from Coober Peedy, called Eric, on display at an Opal Museum in Sydney. (Eric can be seen on my film 'Dowsers Down Under'.)

Could some plesiosauruses have survived until modern times? The Coelacanthe, a primitive fish thought to have been extinct for some 250 million years, was discovered alive and well in Pacific waters. And New Zealand's Tuatara reptile is a lizard-like relic species from 65 million years ago, in an evolutionary branch all of its own. So it is possible.

Australian Water sirens

The Yawk Yawk of western Arnhem Land is a true water spirit, said to live underwater during its youth. Later in life it flies away to live in trees, where it's said to *"make the tree rotten"*. Usually depicted as female, with a fish tail and long strands of algae-like hair, it sometimes walks around on dry land too. Yawk Yawks have husbands and kids and some have ritual importance to the Aborigines. They also enchant mortal men that might fall in love with them, in legend, but it never turns out well at the end. A 'clever man' (shaman) might take one as a wife and perhaps have more luck.

In the Fitzmaurice River region of the Top End, where they are called Murinbungo, there is one such Wardaman legend. A man fell in love with a Murinbungo. He speared and captured her for his own and eventually subdued her feisty ways (by smearing her with his sweat) and they became happy together.

But eventually her sisters lured her back to their river. Her husband searched for her and found her Rainbow Serpent father waiting for him and roaring like thunder. He came back again and found her sunbaking on the shore with her sisters. But on grabbing her she bit him and father appeared menacingly again. The man tried yet again to re-capture her, but on the third attempt the Rainbow Serpent killed him, related Wardaman elder Bill Harney.

New Zealand's Taniwha

New Zealand is a youthful and rugged land of fire and water, borne with much volcanic activity. For the sea-faring Maori, the water element was predominant in their world and thus spirits of water were of primary significance. Spirits of seas, rivers, volcanoes and hot springs are to this day recognised as pre-eminent in Maori mythos.

The mightiest devic denizens of water are known as Taniwha (pronounced tunifa). Found in both salt and fresh waters alike, a Maori writer likens the Taniwha to Eurasian dragons and also the Australian Rainbow Serpent and Bunyip. Certainly the roles they enact have much similarity. Bunyips, related anthropologist Charles Mountford in 1976 - *"live in deep holes in watercourses and they punished, usually with drowning, all who trespassed on their domain."*

Taniwha temperaments were also said to be often ferocious and dangerous, but they could also be fierce guardians of their territory and adopted peoples, the Maori who lived in their domain. There are many stories of heroic battles of early tribes with unfriendly taniwhas, both on land and in the water. Like the European dragon killing legends, the people always win!

Like the Australian Rainbow Serpents, some Taniwhas were said to have created harbours, by opening up channels to the sea. Not for the faint hearted to clairvoyantly observe, Taniwhas manifest in a half-crocodile (or big lizard), half-human form, having a human torso and fearsome croc head. Elsdon, in 1924, wrote that they are generally water- dwelling creatures of saurian form, mostly man slayers or man eaters, while some are perfectly harmless. The Maori say that the Taniwha can be noisy, making bellowing or even roaring sounds. On the ocean a Taniwha may appear as a whale or shark. In rivers and lakes it might appear as big as a whale, or smaller, in the form of a gecko or tuatara. Some individuals were known to assume a range of differing forms.

In some Maori cave drawings we see lizard-like Taniwha. One example, in Hamilton, was made in 1868; others are found in Tangawhai Gorge, South Canturbury. In other Maori art the Taniwha appears in the form of fish-tailed merman figures carved onto meeting houses, which probably represent Taniwha protectors of the tribe.

Taniwhas are usually associated with particular areas, but in one Maori story a Taniwha roamed about until it settled in the Wellington district and ultimately died, in death forming a small island. At Lake Taupo a fierce Taniwha, called Horo-Matangi, resided on the west side of Motutaiko Island in an underwater cave. It was said to manifest as either a reptile, a black rock, or an old man as red as fire. This man is considered to be custodian of the mana of the lake, that was created by a huge volcanic explosion several centuries ago.

Taniwhas could be classified as atua or tipua - supernatural presences, mighty beings with extraordinary powers; and sometimes acting as the mauri (life-force) of the associated human community. Tribes sometimes referred to their great chiefs as Taniwhas. A man closely associated with a Taniwha might even be regarded as one after death. (In China the emperors, in a similar move, likened themselves to the dragon forces of nature and referred to themselves as a dragon.)

Another version of the Taniwha is the Ngarara. These mainly dangerous or evil beings are described as having teeth studded jaws, bat wings, hard scaly skin with rows of spines all down the back, and a long and dangerous tail.

When treated with respect, Taniwhas were usually well behaved towards people. One normally steered clear of their dens, but if passing or fishing nearby one, it was customary to make a propitiary offering. Often this was in the form of a green twig or branch that was offered, while approriate karakia (prayers) were recited.

Only certain types of Taniwha can be appeased with offerings however. Tohunga, the medicine man, would make seasonal offerings to certain taniwha who enjoyed the first kumara or taro of the harvest, or the first bird or fish caught in the season.

A custom around the Manukau Harbour, near Auckland, was to appease the local Taniwha if there was any impending trouble such as illness or war. A small raft with a miniature house fastened to it, in which mullet flesh or some other delicacy would be placed for the Taniwha, would be anchored off-shore overnight. If the food was gone by morning, the Taniwha's help was assured.

Mostly regarded with fear, some families had Taniwhas as kaitiaki - family guardian spirits. Taniwhas could take a liking to certain individuals, families or hapu/sub tribes. When all went well the Taniwhas were great guardians, warning of the approach of enemies, via the interpretations of the tohunga. A Ngarara could be adopted as the pet of a chief, but only if offerings of food were regularly given to keep it happy.

Hamurana Springs, on the northern edge of Lake Rotorua, is a site of great spiritual importance. Here are some fifteen bubbling springs, the largest of which, despite being only spa-pool sized, emits nearly five million litres of water per hour. This main outlet was once the home of a female Taniwha known as Hinerua. She was gentle, unlike other Rotorua Taniwha, and the pet of a local chieftainess. Hinerua would visit her mistress regularly and after her death was never seen again.

Another legend tells of how ancestor Rau Kai Hau Tu would mark a poisonous water pool (common in volcanic areas) by enlisting the help of a friendly Taniwha who would be prevailed upon to stay guarding the site permanently, warning those who came not to drink there.

Taniwha carving (Auckland Museum).

18. Water shrines and healing waters

Springs offering life-sustaining waters were traditionally protected from harm and often honoured with special shrines, placed where the genius locii lurked. A sacred focal point, the water shrine was a central precinct of many early settlements, with ceremonial processional ways leading there. Later, especially in the Middle Ages, healing springs sometimes had pilgrims' huts and sanctuaries built nearby, erected by the grateful.

An amazingly well preserved Neolithic water shrine, dated at 4,700 years as the oldest of its kind, was found in 1995 in the Brecon Beacons in South Wales. A local forest ranger made this rare discovery while digging a pond. Horizontally laid timbers formed a 9m (30 ft) walkway surrounding three sides of a stretch of water 18m (60 ft) by 13.5m (45 ft) long, with a wooden structure on the fourth, eastern side. In the centre of the pond stood a circle of a dozen wooden poles that may have risen to up to 6m (18 ft) above the water. These Oak timbers may once have been connected together by horizontal wooden lintels. If so, the whole thing would have had a *"resemblance to Stonehenge"*, reported The Independent, on 7/12/95. Wet locations are known to have had great significance in those times, and thus the site has been excavated (or some might say desecrated) by members of the local Archeological Trust.

Neolithic religious structures were typically laid out in a circle or oval that was formed from tree trunks or stone megaliths. The circular nature of such ancient shrines suggest the idea of endless cycles, the circle of the seasons and the revolution of celestial bodies. That most well known of great circular temples, Stonehenge in England, (pictured next page) turns out to be also connected to water - the nearby Avon River. In 2006 excavations not far from Stonehenge found a henge, a circle of ditches and earthen banks, at Durrington Walls. This once enclosed concentric rings of huge timber posts, *"basically a wooden version of Stonehenge"*. The new findings include a *"well-trodden avenue from Durrington Walls to the Avon River"* and a village that may have housed Stonehenge's builders and/or semi-nomadic pilgrims of 4,600 years ago. The ruins appear to be the largest Neolithic village ever found in Britain. The roadway is paved with stone and leads to the Avon River, about 150m (160 yd) away. It is very similar to a river road running from Stonehenge to the Avon River.

Julian Thomas, a professor of archaeology at Manchester, thinks that the Durrington Walls timber temple was where midwinter would have been celebrated and much evidence of feasting was found there. Stonehenge appears to have been used for midsummer celebrations, which were more sedate affairs, with no deposits of animal bones and broken pottery. Thomas reported in February 2007 that:

"What this means is that Stonehenge, with its circles of stones, and Durrington Walls, with its circles of timbers, which are directly comparable, are actually linked together by this pair of avenues and the river... Effectively, they're one integrated structure."

Significant to our watery focus, the massive, mainly dolerite, stones of Stonehenge were brought from a mind-boggling 250 miles away, from the Preseli Mountains in south-west Wales. A geochemical study in

1991 was able to accurately determine the stones' origins, National Geographic reported in June 2008. The naturally formed pinnacle stones originally stood in an area where local folklore attributed healing power to the local springs. Once erected in the great circle, the stones also had a reputation for healing, whereby people would drink water that had been poured over them.

Sacred springs

Sacred springs may be found miraculously gushing from harsh rocky hillsides, on high mountain tops and passes, at salty seashores and in peaty bogs. People would once regularly visit them for rituals of healing and problem solving. Often a sacred tree grew beside them and in Europe Ash trees and nymph spirits were closely associated with the springs. Originally, people sought wisdom from the resident nymph who presided over the sacred waters, often after a token of gift giving.

The sacred spring waters were truly fonts of health in those times. When water cleansing treatments were unknown, spring waters provided the purest water available and thus they quickly established curative and restorative, as well as magical, reputations.

The peasant doctor wise ones knew which medicinal herbs could be added to the spring waters to effect their simple folk remedies. Such traditions were kept secret for fear of persecution during the Dark Ages, but they never disappeared completely.

A 16th century Irish book, The Life of St Columcille, mentions many healing wells and tells of the crowds of pilgrims who came in the mid 14th century to St Mullin's Well to pray and walk in the stream waters there. *"Some came through devotion, the majority through fear of the plague,"* a commentator noted. Some wells were even called Tobar na Plaighe – the Well of the Plague.

The sacred waters were visited often and for a range of purposes. They were taken by both man and beast to cure various ills, as well as for psychological problems and infertility. There were also wells used for magic (surviving as 'wishing wells'), as well as for cursing, for affecting the weather, for deflecting storms and attracting rain.

Fishermen on the Isle of Man would visit the Wells of the North or South Wind and give offerings in the hope of procuring favourable winds at sea. Before heading out, they would ritually throw handfuls of water into the air towards the preferred direction of the wind.

An Irish myth, related by Lady Gregory, tells of the Well of the Moon, that: *"whosever would drink of it would get wisdom and after a second drink he would get the gift of foretelling. ...Three daughters of Beag (the owner) had charge of the well and they would not part with a vessel of it for anything less than red gold."*

Like the Well of the Moon, many sacred water sources were considered to be able to impart oracular powers. But water magic isn't always available every day and at Loch na Naire in Sutherland, Scotland, the water was said to only have magical and medicinal qualities between 12am and 1am on Lammas Day (1st August) and May Day (1st May).

Some healing wells were reputed to be helpful in cases of infertility and King James II and his second queen visited St Winefrede's Well at Holywell in Wales in 1686, in the hope of procuring a child. Other wells were renowned for curing particular minor conditions such as warts, rheumatism, whooping cough, skin diseases and backache. Iron rich waters such as the chalybeate springs of the Chalice Well in Glastonbury were often associated with healing. Some wells had a reputation for curing love sickness.

It is curious that a great many healing waters were associated with the curing of eye problems. This has been explained by well researcher Katy Gordan, who wrote that *"people suffered badly from vitamin A deficiency during mediaeval times, and the primary symptom of that is sore eyes"*. Smoky kitchen fires can also cause this problem.

As a cure for mental illness, people used to be tossed into some sacred waters for a bit of shock therapy. At Tobar na n-Gealt, the Well of the Lunatics in Co. Kerry, people drank the clear waters and ate the watercress that grew there. In Scotland the mentally ill were immersed three times in the waters of Loch Maree, or towed around the island by boat. It didn't always work though.

It was always customary at the healing wells to give offerings in gratitude for services rendered. This usually took the form of a piece of rag, a bent pin, nail, needles, coins, flowers, food or drink. Often those seeking cures would tie a rag to clootie trees or shrubs. These can still be seen today in Ireland covered with colourful strips of rag. The rags were traditionally a piece of the clothing of those seeking cures and they symbolised the health problems that were being left behind. These clooties are meant to rot away as the ailment ceased. Unfortunately the clootie trees of today can look very messy, with synthetic rag materials refusing to break down!

Irish clootie tree

Visiting one St Lassairs Well in Roscommon I saw several pens, presumably left to invoke good results in examinations, as thanks for academic assistance. An elderly woman I met there explained how the spring had changed its location due to an incident of blaspheming that had occured long ago, beside it's original location.

The commonest votive offerings at Irish wells today are holy pictures, rosaries and candles. And at St Winefride's Well at Holywell around 50,000 candles a year are burned in a century-old tradition.

At some Roman-Celtic water shrines there was once a brisk trade in models of body parts made from Oak, ivory and copper alloy, or recycled from old statues. These were purchased and flung into the waters in seeking a cure for that body part. At Bath and other Roman water shrines, people would write their problems on lead scrolls and throw them into the water.

To this day, in some quiet country corners, whole communities get involved in decorating their local sacred springs at annual well dressings. The tradition is strong in Derbyshire, England, where the decorations, in the form of arrangements of flowers and greenery, have a Victorian flavour. Indeed the custom was a Victorian era revival.

Traditions of water rituals are also found at Droitwich, Worcester, where dressings of St Richard's well occurred up until the Civil War. When the practice ceased, the waters dried up. When it was revived - the water came back! (A revival of well dressing features in chapter 21.)

Holistic insights

Modern scientific investigations into holy or healing waters of Europe, measuring their electrical fields, have found significant differences between them and the ordinary, non-sacred springs or well waters that were tested.

Traditional healing waters have also been found to be rich in minerals such as germanium, which helps maintain high oxygen levels in the water and is highly therapeutic. The miraculous healing of Catherine Latapie on 1st March 1858 was the first recorded cure at France's Lourdes. These days, 2,500 unexplained healings later, Lourdes water is found to be high in germanium.

As well as minerals and gases in water, the effect of the prayers of pilgrims, their state of meditation and thankfulness at sacred sources, must all contribute energetically, and help to provide the overall curative effects and lovely atmosphere one finds at such places.

The other aspect of the curative functions of these wells, the knowledge most suppressed by the Church, was the presence of powerful water spirits who dispensed loving compassion and healing energies to those who successfully engaged their services, whether consciously requested or not.

Tobernault holy well, Sligo, Ireland

19. Spirit of Water in Christianity

The Biblical Holy Spirit is traditionally feminine, says feminist writer Barbara Walker. Personified by the white dove and, as ruach in Biblical and Hebrew traditions, she hovers or broods over the waters as a creative mist. Sometimes described as weather or wind, a storm or a whirlwind, the word ruach combines meanings of breath, mind and spirit, and is similar to the Greek concept of pneuma. Sometimes ruach is identified as *"air, gas from the womb"*.

Examples of water magic and healing are found in the Bible. The ability of water to be divinely energised, conditioned by devic influence, is also in there and such concepts are a continuation of older, animist traditions. Holy water might be found in churches, but no church has a monopoly over sacred waters!

Particularly evocative is the Biblical description of the pool of Bethesda, of when *"an angel went down at a certain season into the pool and troubled the water; whosoever then first after the troubling of the water stepped in was made whole of whatsoever disease he had."*

A similar image was seen by clairvoyant vision above a newly made lake on my property in Victoria. An angelic being, reminiscent of the ruach, was observed by two friends independently and on separate occasions. Dove shaped, and several metres across, it was hovering over the surface of the water (which had, amazingly, filled in its first fortnight, during a drought). Looking like a hummingbird at a flower, its head focusing intently downwards from its station, a beam of energy projected down from it's forehead into the water. I guess this was its way of 'troubling the waters', of charging them up with its power, knowledge and other subtle qualities.

Despite great efforts to stamp out old animist traditions, many ancient water rituals continued to flourish in disguised forms under the banner of Christianity. Certainly the reverence for water was deeply ingrained. In 1704 an act of parliament forbade the practice of 'well worship' and well pilgrimages in Ireland, with a penalty of a public whipping or ten shilling fine. In 1770 a curate of Bromfield in England also decreed all pagan ceremonies at his local Hellywell spring to be banned.

But well and fountain worship continued to prove difficult to eradicate in Europe. It had been popular throughout the Middle Ages and it survived the Reformation.

In fact, a great majority of the sacred wells, in Ireland at least, are found located close by the ruins of medieval parish churches. As these were the central focus of authority in their time it is not surprising that a good supply of drinking water needed to be close by.

Pioneer geomantic researcher Alfred Watkins, in the UK in the 1920s, also rediscovered that there were alignments of all sorts of ancient structures associated with the locations of wells. The alignments (so-called 'ley lines') he found typically run between sighting points such as prominent hills, or *"sometimes from a holy well to a hill and vice-versa"*. (The design of cities, too, was influenced by the presence of sacred water sources, such as the Fleet River in London, as researcher David Furlong discovered.)

Some churches were even built right over an old sacred well and early Celtic churches used them for baptism, until the Roman church replaced their use with a font inside the building. Old churches with a crypt or grotto containing a subterranean spring can still be found here and there. Examples are at Holybourne Church in Hampshire and St Bride's in Fleet Street, London, the latter probably once a spring dedicated to the goddess Bride/Bridget.

Holy water is not the same water as holy well water. Holy water is blessed by priests for use in certain rites, such as the Easter Vigil, at blessings, dedications, exorcisms and burials, etc. It may have originated from an ordinary tap. The custom of sprinkling people with such water at mass began in the 9th century. At this time 'stoups', or fonts of holy water from which people could sprinkle themselves on entering a church, were in common use.

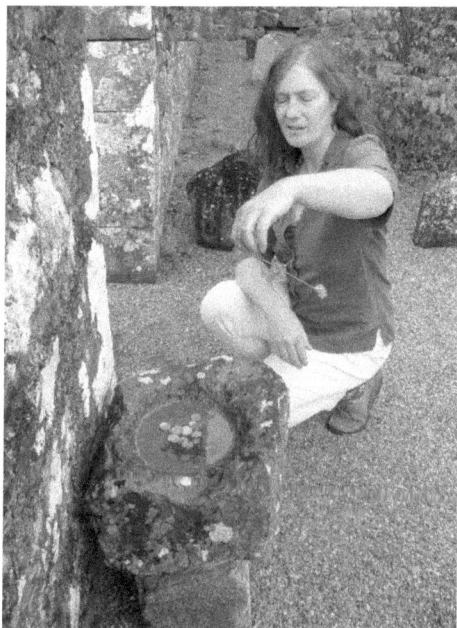

The author dowses powerful energies of a holy water font at a ruined Irish church.

While underground waters were once thought to be empowered by the sun at night, later, in Christian times, water was sometimes charged up energetically by contact with holy relics of saints. These would often be dipped into water for a homoeopathic or placebo effect.

The most recent known cure from such a tradition was in 1963, when holy relics were dipped into the fountain at Le Grand Andeley in Normandy during the vigil and feast of St Clothilde, and sick people were immersed in the water afterwards. The tradition is largely forgotten nowadays and the fountain has degenerated into a simple Wishing Well.

It all harks back to earlier times, when folk healers knew well the art of placing special stones, such as quartz crystal ('the stone of the sun') and other gems, as well as medicinal herbs, into sacred waters to impart healing energies. The tradition continues today in various forms, such as the vibrational healing modalities of gem, shell and flower essences.

*The sacred fish and tree are Christian symbols from Biblical times.
But these familiar symbols were actually preceeded by those of ancient
cultures, as seen in this Indian stone carving (British Museum).*

20. Irish Well pilgrimages

In old Ireland there were once at least 3,000 sacred wells, springs and pools. Here they are found in a much greater concentration than anywhere else in the world. Many of these were ancient sites of pilgrimage. Popular times to visit these water sources were at the special festival dates of the year, such as Imbolc on February 1st, Beltaine on May 1st, summer solstice on June 21-22nd, Lughnasa on August 1st and Samhain on November 1st.

These turning-points of the Celtic year were deemed to be times when the veils between other worlds were opened. It was a time for visions, communication with the spirit world and divine inspiration. Later, in Christian times, the dates and names of the festivals were changed a bit, but the original pagan practise of honouring the waters prevailed in thinly disguised form.

Mainly a feature of the Catholic countries, the tradition of sacred pilgrimage continued up until the Middle Ages and, in England, well into late medieval times. It later enjoyed a revival of interest there in the 17th and 18th centuries. After the Reformation the largest stronghold of spiritual pilgrimage tradition remaining was in Ireland. It is still practiced there today, but on a much smaller scale.

The Irish pilgrimage, the 'pattern day' or 'turas', focuses on a particular complex of sacred sites and objects, and usually features a holy well. A variety of 'stations' are visited on a certain day or time of year, and these are 'rounded' or circumnavigated, while prayers are chanted. Pilgrims 'doing the rounds' drink from the well and may touch, kiss or rub themselves with sacred stones, according to a set pattern.

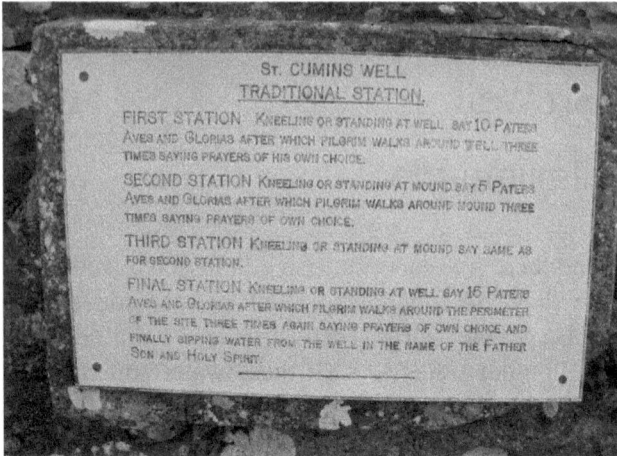

Pilgrims were often required to pray kneeling or to make their way around the stations on their bare knees, often a painful procedure!

Interestingly, the energy centres (chakras) in the kneecaps are fantastic points for energy reception. When I first began sensing the presence of the devas I would often receive an energy zap from them in my knees. Perhaps the ancient act of kneeling while praying stimulates those points, making pilgrims more receptive to the magic of place?

The author at St Cumins Well, Co. Mayo, Ireland.

The Irish and British well pilgrimages became important social occasions, especially on Sundays and the feast days of saints associated with them. Every district in Ireland had its saint whose name and legends were attached to various topographical features and who replaced the original deities of place, taking over from archaic heroes and well nymphs.

Ireland's vernacular saints have been described as the genius loci, *"...the spirit of place itself, more accessible and homelier than remote divinities"*, writes Stiofan O' Cadhla.

Many wells are dedicated, or indeed 'owned' by the local saint. St Bridget's Wells are many and there are many 'St Bridgets'! Irish goddess Bridgid (Bride in the UK) presided over healing, medicine, smithcraft and poetry. She carried a famous cauldron, which was no doubt a prototype of the so-called 'Holy Grail'.

Bridget's name refers to brightening days of spring. On her feast day of February 1st, the first day of spring, Bridget Crosses are made for her in the shape of quartered circles – sun symbols. As well as being associated with sacred wells and perhaps the ancient tradition of the underground sun, St Bridget's name and attributes are much like those of Sulis, and so she is the major successor of the vernacular well nymphs and goddesses.

But this isn't always the case, as author Patrick Logan discovered, recalling the St Bridget pilgrimage held in his home town in County Leitrim. Logan would join pilgrims in reciting the rosary, while approaching the local cemetery. Here they walked three times around an old Ash Tree and later knelt beside a carved stone supposed to represent the head of St Bridget. In the 1970s this stone was excavated and cleaned and found to have a beard!

Many wells were associated with St Patrick and legends tell how the saint displaced druids who had been in charge of them. Patrick blessed the sacred sources in the name of Christianity and then used the water to baptise converts. Some legends tell of a well miraculously appearing, in response to his command.

Or, in the case of the well that is now hidden below the edge of Nassau Street in central Dublin, beneath the entrance to Trinity College, its waters was said to be brackish until St Patrick's magical prayers made them sweet and pure again. No doubt more invented propaganda!

St Patrick's feast day is 17th March and this is when some of his wells are visited for patterns/turas. However often his name has supplanted an earlier saint whose feast day was at other times.

Other wells are visited on Trinity Sunday in early June, Easter, or May Eve or May Day, the beginning of summer. The midsummer feast of 24th June, now the festival of St John the Baptist, was another popular feast day in Ireland. Ancient midsummer rituals began at sunset of the day before, high up on hill tops where fires were lit. People sometimes waited around wells for the midnight hour, when tradition had it that the water 'boiled up' and was capable of curing any ill.

Most of the subsequent Christian festivals that occur between 22nd July and 15th August were designed to replace the Lughnasa festivals that originally celebrated the beginning of harvest and the agricultural deities. The last Sunday in July, for instance, is the pattern day at the holy well of Tobernalt, near Sligo, (seen in the following photos) and mass is said there twice that day. There are fourteen praying stations

around this beautiful sacred grove and well area, some of which are merely piles of small stones. Each is numbered with Roman numerals, to represent the stations of the cross in a Catholic church, which the ritual replicates.

There are few festival dates for well pilgrimages occuring later than harvest time. One was held on St Martin's Day, November 11th, when a black cockeral was traditionally killed and its blood sprinkled in the corners of the home. But generally the cold half of the year was unsuitable for outdoor gatherings.

The old pattern days often became racy affairs after dark, by which time piety was done away with. There was plenty of dancing, singing, feasting and love making. A great description of such an event can be found in an 1840 book Holy Wells of Ireland (which is available as a free download from the internet). Author Father Charles O'Connor, enquiring about the well at Beer Crowcombe in Somerset and the early 20th-century gatherings there was told that:

"The well had the property of bubbling or moving, even steaming on some well known days of the year, notably Whit Sunday and during the fortnight following. At this time, while waiting the moving of the waters, a rendezvous of the youth and maidens from the villages round took place... There seems to have been a good deal of horse play around the well."

The annual patterns had become important events of social interaction, but often the heady mix of alcohol and testosterone saw them ending with fights, sometimes of a factional nature. A Popery Act of 1704 banned the *"riotous and unlawful assembling together of many thousands of papists to said wells"*.

The festivities were worrying the authorities, who were really waging a war of cultural imperialism and genocide, and for whom the pattern represented a *"sign of Irish anarchy, lawlessness and irreligion"*, says O' Cadhla.

When O'Connor enquired of people why they attended well pilgrimages, a very old man told him that the people continue the tradition because: *"their ancestors always did it, that it was a preservative against Geasu-Draoidacht, i.e. the sorceries of Druids; that their cattle were preserved by it, from infections and disorders; that the daoini maethe, i.e. the fairies, were kept in good humour by it; and so thoroughly persuaded were they of the sanctity of those pagan practices that they would travel bareheaded and barefooted from ten to twenty miles for the purpose of crawling on their knees round these wells, and upright stones and Oak trees westward as the sun travels, some three times, some six, some nine, and so on, in uneven numbers until their voluntary penances were completely fulfilled."*

21. Restoring well traditions in Malvern, England

Geomancy of Malvern

The famous spa centre of the Malvern Hills has attracted visitors for hundreds, if not thousands, of years, for it's beautiful scenery and its reviving waters, particularly during the 18th and 19th centuries. Its location, nestled in bluebell covered hills running like a steep and narrow north-south spine in the region where the borders of Herefordshire, Worcestershire and Gloucestershire converge, provides a scenic backdrop for the revival of well traditions there. All remnant traditions of honouring the waters had died out by the 1970s, but a swag of attractively dressed wells were on display when I visited Malvern on the May Day weekend of 2008. And the expanses of sweet smelling bluebells beneath the forest trees were the best seen in years!

The nine mile long range of the Malvern Hills is comprised of ancient granite peaks, encircled by a necklace of pure water springs, which mostly occur where the granite meets lower sedimentary rock layers. The once famous springs are numerous, but nowadays most are malingering in various states of decay and neglect. However when I visited there were 32 wells that had been embellished with colourful decorations of all kinds, in a modern festival of well dressing.

The Hills themselves have a dramatic pull for modern people on pilgrimage, such as members of the Gatekeeper Trust. Their geomantic appreciation of the place has likened the form of the hills to a gigantic sleeping Earth Mother goddess, with a series of hilltop chakras running down her body on the range of peaks. The most famous of Malvern's wells, St Anne's, is nestled between the goddess's 'breasts', the twin peaks of the Worcestershire Beacon and North Hill.

At the sole of this goddess's right foot lies the Valley of the White Leafed Oak and both sites are a great delight to visit. The famed tree has the most enormous girth in an Oak tree that I have ever seen. It was bedecked with ribbons and other assorted gifts fluttering in the breeze, but unfortunately was in a state of serious health decline, with gaping holes where branches had fallen, a hollow-looking interior and very few leaves; it was struggling to survive.

As for St Anne's Well, it is tucked into a little forest nook on the hillside with a café operating beside it. On the day of my visit a team of Morris Dancers were busily entertaining the crowd in the sunny glade. It has been suggested that the name Anne could actually be a corruption of Welsh/Celtic tan, which means a fire or beacon. St Anne is often associated with flattened hilltops where ancient beacon fires were once located. The well is beside such a flat promontory site, and below this, at 'St Anne's Delight', ritual beacons were once lit. So perhaps it was once called Tan's Hill? Or perhaps St Anne perpetuates the memory of an ancient sun/fire goddess?

Above the well, Worcestershire Beacon towers high in the range and evidence of fire ritual held there around 3,000 years age has come to light in the form of a Bronze Age cremation urn discovered buried on the peak. During my first night's sleep not far from the peak I had a lucid dream of fires spontaneously lighting themselves, of me trying to put them out, but of no menace felt, nor danger arising from them. The next day I read Rose Garrard's book about Malvern's springs and found out about the ancient beacons. It felt to me then, that the dream was about the Spirit of Fire (personified there as the local angel of landscape) which was wanting to reassert itself again in the beacons. Indeed, I was able to dowse, from below, what I perceived to be an enormous fire spirit stationed on the hilltop there. Workshop students the following day were also able to tune into that mighty presence, a firey landscape angel. It was not surprising to find it there, as fire spirits are often found in association with granite areas, the rock being formed under great heat.

The goddess's 'heart chakra' location is said to be the Wyche Cutting, where the road cuts across the ridge to the other side of the range. Nearby is the 'Pixie Path' and the area was once known as the legendary home of the 'little people'. However they were said to have abandoned the vicinity when quarrying began in the 19th century. Numerous quarry sites have scarred the sides of the hills, but are not mined anymore and I'm sure the 'little people' would have returned again by now, but didn't have time to check.

The art of sacred landscape revival

Artist Rose Garrard was born in Greater Malvern but was living in London when she went to Canada to take up a short-term position as an artist in residence. There she met an indigenous Canadian woman who told her of the negative effect of English missionaries on her people in the past and how, in more recent times, one of the greatest tragedies of her people has been the selling of their water rights. Despite this, her tribe were following a path of self-determination once more and didn't appreciate offers of assistance from outside. She encouraged Garrard to go home to her own birthplace and find out about, and protect, the sacred waters there.

She took this suggestion on board and returned to her hometown of Malvern. In 1996 Garrard successfully proposed to the Malvern Hills District Council it's very own 'Spring Water Project'. Thus the following year she embarked on an artist's residency whereby she began researching the history of the springs and went on to design a sculpture trail to celebrate them. As a result, and with much community input, over 100 wells, springs and pools were mapped out and their histories and legends recorded.

Garrard had had a life long interest in sculpture, rituals, folklore, feminism and ecology. In 1998 she began work on her first sculpture for the trail, in the small town park in the centre of Greater Malvern. This renewed a public drinking spout that had been languishing for 30 years. Local residents chose the name Malvina for the carved stone goddess figure she installed there, naming it after a local Celtic priestess.

Malvina

In 1999 the well was 'dressed' (decorated) as part of the May Day festivities, a revival of ancient traditions of honouring the waters. At an adjacent site the new Enigma Fountain was completed in 2000. But sadly the project then ground to a halt, as a result of a change of council after the local elections. The rest of the project was scrapped.

But Garrard stayed on, continuing to work for the restoration of more of the springs in a voluntary capacity. In 1998 she and other determined people formed the Malvern Spa Association and by 2001 they had launched the annual well dressing festival, to coincide with traditional May Day festivities.

Ancient celebrations of life

May Day celebrations of nature go back to ancient times and were enjoyed across the country. In Garrard's childhood in the Malverns she remembers, around 50 years ago, such local customs as the crowning of a youthful May King and Queen, as well as school-aged children dancing around the Maypole. She was once taken to Kent to see a parade of dozens of May Kings and Queens from all the nearby districts coming to be judged to determine the supreme regents of the year. Carrying garlands of flowers, they were dressed fabulously, as elves, pixies, fairies, and as Robin Hoods with their entourage of merry men all dressed in green. Sadly, these traditions have now all died out.

As for well dressing, the definition is *"to cleanse, to put in good order, to prepare, to make straight, to clothe, array, trim."* It certainly sounded like an appropriate thing to do and an activity Garrard also believed that went beyond mere decoration. It was a joyful expression of old spiritual beliefs.

The most well known location for well dressing in the UK is around the Peak district of Derbyshire, where the creation of religious pictures from flower petals continues a tradition begun in 1820. It harks back to much earlier traditions, to at least 1348, at the time of the Black Death, when good, clean water was held in very high esteem as a curative. Malvern's waters are also very pure, and numerous signs displayed at the dressed wells stated that the water is famous for *"containing nothing at all!"* Evidence of well dressing traditions in Malvern go back some 800 years.

Holy Well

My favourite of the Malvern wells is Holy Well on Wells Road, pictured next page. It's a highly revered site which, since medieval times at least, has had people visiting for health cures. It corresponds to the 'sacral chakra' of the Hills, in the goddess scenario.

In the 18th and 19th centuries the 'water cure' was very much in vogue and in 1843 a quaint little building was erected over this well. The 'cure' included treatments such as being wrapped in a cold wet sheet and then doused with the chilly water. Queen Victoria visited Holy Well as a child and stayed a while in the area, thus causing its popularity to soar.

Holy Well became a commercial bottling plant in the 1960's. In the 1970's, after the plant was moved elsewhere, the well was restored for public use and again cures were reported from those who visited to drink it's waters. The current owners are restoring the building and people are living in it, directly above the well. I imagine it would be a challenging location, not energetically suited for habitation.

Dowsing the waters

On the ground floor of this building, where Holy Well (actually a fast running spring-fed stream) has its own little room, the atmosphere is most sublime and it induced me to spend a while there in meditation. The water's energy field was intense and it spilled out and down along the road. Measuring this life-force, in a bottle of Holy Well water at my dowsing workshop the next day, students found its energy to just about fill the entire West Malvern Village Hall!

When the class attuned to a (very poorly) dressed well that had been incorporated into a stone wall in a West Malvern church ground, (seen below) we were able to dowse the presence of a well nymph stationed there. The well waters were dirty and a bit stagnant, and the energy felt pretty sad. One woman bravely pulled out some rubbish, which turned out to contain a dead rat that had been floating around. We sent some love into the water after that. Then I gave a special offering, singing a sacred water song that I had written for such an occasion.

After this the energy of the water radiated out much refreshed and more vibrant, we were able to determine by dowsing. It felt so much better! An expanded water spirit enveloped us in its energetic fold and we felt blessed in return.

Resurgence of the springs

Many of Malvern's wells have been forgotten or displaced over time, sometimes as a result of people attempting to divert them into their own backyards. The Coca Cola company continues to extract vast amounts of spring water for bottling (having purchased a local bottling firm), but have been kept in check by the Spa Association. (The company have an internationally bad reputation for being very greedy with their water extractions!) With help from the Association and funding from the Heritage Lottery Fund 14 spring sites have been restored up to 2006.

The British Society of Dowsers national office was located for a few years in Greater Malvern. In 2005 the Spa Association held a workshop in association with the Water Divining group of the BSD. One of its objects was to locate two missing wells, St Agnes and Hay Well. Two diviners both found and agreed upon the locations of both wells. At that moment a local fellow from next door leaned over his fence and said to them: *"If you are looking for a well - you are on the right spot. A few months ago a wheel of a lorry sank into it!"*

Children dressed this Malvern well.

22. The Spirit of Water in today's world

Mary, the great water spirit

In the current era the Spirit of Water still takes the form of the Great Mother. Indigenous people know Her well. In one of Her most widespread manifestations, She has assumed the character of the spiritual being Mother Mary, with millions of devotees worldwide.

The Biblical Mary has little to do with this great being, a deva who has evolved over the last several thousand years (just as we are all evolving!). The name Mary is a word for the sea and the marine environment, where maricultures are practiced. Mother Mary is sometimes referred to as the 'Star of the Sea'. An earlier goddess – Isis, she of a thousand names - was called Mere in her sea goddess form; Hathor also had this same title. Mary has inherited the attributes of several earlier goddesses, it appears.

Like all tertiary level devas (- the highest!) She can be anywhere and everywhere. Mary often manifests to little children or clairvoyants as a gentle and compassionate blue-white or silver being or energy field, and she is often encountered at holy wells or springs such as Lourdes. She enjoys human interaction and, invariably, Her messages implore contactees to send up more prayer to Her. This would add to Her personal power base and help facilitate the many miracles attributed to Mary since Her cult began.

In Ireland well pilgrimage traditions go in and out of fashion, but often it is Mary who provides a thread of continuum to modern times. For instance in 1985 in County Waterford, Ireland, a holy well was revealed, in a vision, near a Cistercian monastery at Mount Melleray. A statue of Mary had been placed at a site in a verdant little valley. Afterwards, writes Janet Bord: *"one night a glowing light lit up the stream from the spring"*. There were several visions of Mary and messages were given to pray more and to recognise that the water was blessed. A shelter for visitors and a 'Lourdes Grotto' were later erected.

In South Australia, the Anglican Church or Our Lady of Yankalilla was the scene of a series of Mary visions and phenomena during the 1990s. It became a pilgrimage centre for people from far and wide, many of whom received healing. (I have written about this in greater detail in my book Divining Earth Spirit.) Holy water is drawn from beneath the church and bottled there for pilgrims.

The church site itself is located over the top of an Aboriginal sacred site. This was also the scene of a terrible massacre of the local Aboriginals, when people of all ages were killed. An odd site for a church to be placed!

But when I visited and tuned in to the energies of place, there was no sense of any 'bad vibes' from the massacre. Several water spirits were detected in the church and the atmosphere was delightful.

I would think that the effect of thousands of pilgrims' prayers plus Mary's compassionate energy has soothed the pain. The loving-wisdom of the Spirit of the Waters has attracted what was necessary to help to heal the site.

'Our Lady of the Fenceposts'

Sightings of Mother Mary on the northern headland of Coogee Beach were first reported in the media in December 2002. It seems to have started off as a trick of the eye. Along a whitewashed fence line, at a certain hour in the afternoon on sunny days, a white, veiled figure would appear. The play of fence angles and shadows is said to have produced the image, which had never been noticed before.

Dowsing the apparition site at Coogee Beach

People began flocking to the site to witness this 'apparition' for them selves and to pray there. But the phenomena wasn't just a feature of the fencepost site. Several people reported seeing Mary in different spots around the fence, such as in cliff caves below. Other types of visions were occurring, spirit voices were heard and spiritual epiphanies and healing miracles ensued for some of the pilgrims. These continue to this day.

In February 2005 newspapers reported that some people were demanding a shrine be built at the fence post site, which by then, was a colourful jungle of statues in a little garden, with flowerpots, a holy water bowl, Virgin Mary pictures and laminated press clippings attached to the fence.

While of the belief that it's all just an optical illusion, Coogee parish priest Fr Desmond Holm had seen it's therapeutic value. Holm said in a newspaper report that:

"People have said that it is a special place, that being there gives them a general sense of peace and that is something good. ...If good comes out of it, then that's good."

Looking at the site with my own geomantic perspective (with fresh eyes on an old childhood haunt) reveal it to be a special 'landscape temple' complex, a network of power centres, both on land and out to sea. Truly a modern sacred site in-the-making.

To fully appreciate the site and its Earth mysteries, one needs to look at the site's history, as well as be able to dowse or somehow directly sense the energies there. A history of the phenomena follows.

Just weeks before the apparitions began, on October 12th, 2002, Kuta Beach in Bali suffered the horror of bomb blasts. Hundreds were killed, including 22 who came from the Coogee area. At some point in the following months it was proposed to create a memorial in the parkland above the beach, on the northern headland of Coogee Bay.

This was duly carried out and April 12th 2003 saw the dedication of Coogee's memorial to all Australians killed in the blast, at a ceremony where thousands of mourners vented their grief. In the form of an elegant metal sculpture, it became a sacred memorial where remembrance ceremonies are held annually.

My first brief geomantic investigation of the site was on 27/10/03. It was a windy day for dowsing and I gained no sense of special energies there. But I did see the white figure at the fence, and it made me gasp with surprise!

More became apparent when I returned on 15/3/04. At the ad hoc fencepost shrine I chatted with a man who had been praying intently with his rosary. He told me how, on 1/2/03 he had seen a small Mary figure, like a doll with outstretched hands, appear to him there. Nuns were all around him praying at the time and Mary even spoke to him.

But if there had been special energies there, they were still not yet apparent to me on my short visits. However on that day as I was leaving I was able to see, looking out to the Bay beyond the fence shrine, a vortex, shimmering up in the air there.

"Ahha!" I thought, *"that must be where Mary makes her entrance"* (a vortex being capable of acting as a portal or inter-dimensional doorway) … *"and that is why She doesn't manifest up at the memorial. She visits via the nearest suitable Earth energy vortex."*

Checking a geological map, we deepened our understanding of the energies of place. There were thin intrusion lines and points of volcanic basalt rock, all consistent with the pattern of subtle energy hot spots!

When I next visited I came with clairvoyant colleague Billy Arnold. It was 16/10/04, four days after the second anniversary of the Kuta bombing. Wreaths lay fading in the sunlight beneath the commemorative plaque on the remains of the old Bath House entrance, not far from the fencepost shrine.

This time we both looked for devic activity and were delighted to discover a huge green and blue deva presiding over the headland. A giant energy field of devic consciousness, it was peacefully stationed there, full of compassion and healing qualities, and hosting a range of other spirits in it's wings, including an old Earth spirit and several ancestral Aboriginal spirits. There were also two big sea spirits, as well as resident Banksia and other tree spirits in the vicinity that Billy was able to clairvoyantly see.

Billy reported that: *"the big spherical blue-green devic being is at peace there, working for the benefit of living humans and the dead. It likes to be looked at and responds by directing energy to us and to other people nearby. It's difficult to perceive the whole spirit when in a meditative state at the fence post, as you are actually standing in it."*

We next visited together a year later, on 22/10/05, and were blown away by the increased energy of the site. Again, it was not long after an annual commemoration ceremony had occurred and floral wreaths in the Bath House marked the occasion. The energy was really building!

The whole place had a vibrancy we had never felt before. Plants and trees were flourishing, glistening even, and a couple of small flocks of cockatoos and ravens hopped around happily. Shiny black ravens were hanging around the fencepost shrine like guardians, caaaawing merrily. Billy observed the same huge spherical being and it was much larger than the year before. He said that: *"It's covering all of Coogee Bay and the northern headland now. It's very, very impressive and definitely evolving into a much more sophisticated and multi-dimensional being, because of the natural development in the groups of human spirits and nature spirits involved, I imagine."*

We visited again on the Monday afterwards, October 25th. It was a damp, misty day, with sparse visitors. Moist, mysterious and peaceful. Sitting in the car facing the site I undertook an intensive dowsing session, a question and answer interview with the great deva, trying to learn more about this intriguing place.

From this dowsing, assuming my questions were not too flawed, I learnt that the big (female) deva is basically a sea spirit, a bit like a mermaid, whose tail connects down behind the fencepost shrine, via the vortex I had perceived, into the waters of Coogee Bay.

I was able to distantly dowse where the deva's tail connects into an Earth energy centre out to sea. Billy's later discovery, on geological maps, was consequently not surprising at all. Coogee Bay was the scene of volcanic activity long ago, he found. So there are certainly some high energy zones out there!

I asked the deva, on a hunch, if she had once been stationed at Wedding Cake Island, not far off shore. Yes, indeed she had, was the answer. Nowadays she prefers the atmosphere of the headland and has taken on healing work under the tutelage of Mother Mary, who visits occasionally, by popular request.

Before the Bali bombing this great deva of all the Bay was always interested in the welfare of swimmers and surfers at Coogee Beach, I discovered, and now her healing abilities had grown exponentially. People who have been drinking from the holy water container at the fence post had reported cures, as noted in press clippings on display there. After my dowsing session, Billy took a clairvoyant look at the site and was amazed to perceive the spherical spirit as so much more powerful than on the Friday before, with brighter colours and energy radiating in every direction.

He said that: *"Not only were its blue and green colours brighter, it now has flashes of gold and white, like lightning bolts, inside it's field. I think this spirit must be evolving rapidly from the sentiment and emotion of people attending the site on the weekend before, perhaps."*

We walked on up through the old Banksia trees gracing the headland and over to the Bali memorial. The powerful devic field there was quite palpable and exhilarating to experience. It is definitely a sacred site I would recommend for regular visitation, attunement and enjoyment.

Meanwhile, at a suburban home in Fremantle, Western Australia in recent years, a statue of Mary has been shedding tears of compassion in response to the many pilgrims who visit it. When taken to a troubled Aboriginal community in the Northern Territory, it caused a great outpouring of renewed peacefulness and civic pride.

23. Meetings with river deities

A meeting on the River Thames

In September 2007 I was traveling home from Ireland when a storm severely disrupted plane schedules and I missed my long-haul flight. I had an unscheduled stop in London for 24 hours and stayed over with a friend near the Thames River. It turned out to be a magic day!

I had not long before been given, by dowsers in Sweden, two special energy balls, one packed with healing frequencies intended for the benefit of earth elemental beings, the other for water spirits. I could relicate them at will. It seemed like a good idea to offer them to any important devas I could find on my 'day off'.

I map dowsed the best destination to do this and was soon walking in the warm sunshine towards the selected spot in a corner of Battersea Park, beside the Thames. I was very relaxed and open to meetings with the devic world. As I wandered along the river walk I saw that ahead of me the riverbank was largely bare, except for a wild patch of vegetation beside the path, next to the bridge. That seemed to be the most natural location for connecting to any water spirits that might be out in the river.

To faciltate this work I have a deva helper, who travels around with me and networks with the local devas of place. I asked if he could find some important water devas and to tell them that I would be offering them a gift, if we could all rendezvous together at that point at 2pm. This gave us all plenty of time to get there and also time for some meditation at the beautiful Buddhist Peace Pagoda further along the riverbank (pictured next page).

Soon I was sitting on the grass meditating beside the big pagoda for a

short spell of blissful peace. But then disturbing sounds of gardeners with a noisy truck close by forced me to open my eyes. I was a bit shocked to see what the gardener gang were up to - pulling up all the little flowers from the garden beds around the pagoda, these being in perfect condition and of vibrant beauty. I could sense the flowers' shock and pain and the atmosphere went from peaceful to panicked.

I closed my eyes again and changed my meditation, focussing on the flower spirits that were about to be torn out. I warned them what was about to happen and suggested that they detach themselves from their flowers and find somewhere else to live, rather than be driven away in the back of the truck and dumped. Then I headed off towards the nearby river, as 2pm was approaching.

Walking slowly along the path I became aware that there was a trail of little flower spirits following along behind me. They had bailed out of their beds and must have assumed that I would know a good place to move to. So I lead my invisible entourage forward, finally stopping at the riverbank wall from where I could look out over the mighty River Thames.

My senses were heightened by the meditation and devic contacts made. I could perceive something approaching, it looked like a gigantic white swan floating down the river. I realised that it was an other-dimensional throne with swan-wing-like sides. In the middle of it sat what looked like, what must be, the regal duo of god and goddess of the river. They were sailing slowly, gliding along in their majestic craft towards that wild patch of trees on the riverbank, where I was heading also.

Arriving at our rendezvous point, I jumped over the wall and sat down beneath a tree whose branches bent down so low that some of them were touching the water. There I was concealed from the idle eyes of passers by and I instructed the little flower spirits to also come in, suggesting that if they stayed there they would be safe from interference.

I then became aware of a huge outstreched hand reaching over to me from the river. The deities wanted their gift! I replicated my water energy ball, with an act of willpower, and held it out in my two hands towards them. As the ball was taken, my hands felt lighter. I then sensed radiant delight at the energy being received, as well as the gratitude of the great river beings. For my part, I was buzzing and happy to have missed my flight!

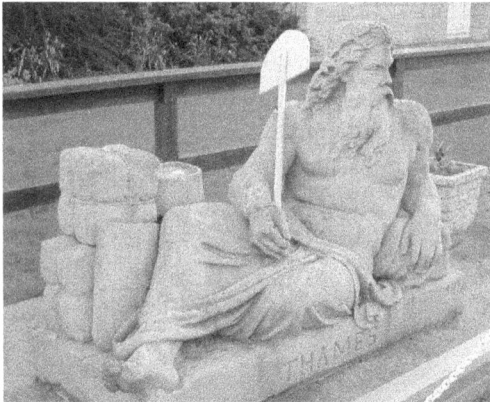

Father Thames is the traditional deity of the River Thames. This statue of him is at St John's Lock, Lechlade, Gloucerstershire. Mother Thames has been long forgotten, I suppose.

Dowsing Irish river serpents

Over in Ireland I believe I have also met up with the great spirit of the River Shannon, at a hidden corner called World's End, not far from Limerick city. I was surprised, considering the presence of a nearby hydro-electric station, that She was still so powerful! Manifesting as a spherical devic field that was hovering across the river, She responded joyfully to my offering to Her - my sacred water song, on that occasion.

Oral traditions give this devi a serpentine form, which is not surprising, considering the perseverance of legends and the evidence of dowsing. A connection between rivers and serpent beings appears in an old tale about the River Dinin, near Kilkenny, as related by Mairie Mac Neill. She says that this river *"no doubt because of its turbulence, has an unfavourable reputation in tradition. It is accursed."* The local Jenkinstown region was once a stronghold of pagan traditions, necessitating a bit of one-up-manship from St Patrick and providing a rare insight to the nature of the water spirits. One old folk tale of the River Dinin has it *"that St Patrick cursed its stones"*. Another tells us that he *"metamorphosed a piast (a serpent) into this river."*

Back at the River Shannon my dowsing has revealed the presence of a serpentine energy form following the river's path. The powerful meandering energy can be detected flowing down the centre. This flow seems to denote an energetic form of the river goddess's body and helps to explain why St Patrick was so keen to have Ireland rid of its 'snakes', so emblematic of the old gods and goddesses.

The snake-like energy line still flows down the entire length and goddess Sionnan meets sea god Manannan at the Shannon Mouth, despite the energetic hazards of passing by metal bridges and hydro-electric power stations inbetween, I was surprised to discover. (The yang serpent line of the River Fergus also joins Sionnan there.)

Ancient Romans were wise to the problem of metals interrupting a river's energy flow. Their River Tiber, ruled by the god Tiberinus, was protected from this hazard by a decree that banned the building of metal bridges over it.

In the case of the Shannon I suspect that the serpent deva has been smart enough to avoid this sort of energetic insult. My dowsing enquiry finds that She dives deep to avoid disturbing energies. The old stone bridges on this river also help to maintain its natural energetic integrity.

24. Honouring water

Developing spiritual relationship with water

The Spirit of Water may nowadays often be ailing, but her powers can be reclaimed. When we reawaken to and cherish the blessings that water brings, humankind and the planet will more likely be sustained. A sustainable relationship with water is one of mutual respect and understanding. Looking back at old traditions can be a guide to better relations with water in the future.

In ancient times the Finns and Saami people of northern Europe showed great respect and sensitivity to water with some beautiful traditions. In that culture the Spirit of Water was called Mere-Ama, Vete-Ema or Mier-Iema, the Sea Mother. (She also resides in fresh waters.) People honoured Her at ceremonies where they splashed each other with water. If they were to gain the blessings of the Water Mother, then good health and fertility, for people, livestock and vegetation would be assured.

When a woman married and moved to a new home one of her first duties was to make herself known to the local Mere-Ama, the Water Mother of the area. She would go to the nearest stream and give offerings of bread and cheese, or cloth and thread, and also wash her face in the waters or sprinkle herself with them.

I think that anyone moving to a new area would also do well to become acquainted with the local water spirits. Find them, introduce yourself to them and show them that you care about them. It doesn't matter much how you do it. When you open yourself to the possibility of the spirit world all sorts of amazing things can happen. I have a strong sense that the Spirit of Water really does want us to make these connections and that harmony can be restored through the healing and connecting powers of water.

A lovely, true story illustrates this well. I once met a woman who lived alone, far from her original home and she was craving for a partner in her life. A wild little stream ran past her home and I introduced her to an important Water Mother spirit who resided there. Some months after I left I had some lovely correspondence about the aftermath of my brief visit. The woman told me that: *"through dowsing I was able to pinpoint the area the deva originated from and entered into dialogue with it"*.

Later on she met a wonderful man who she eventually married. Unfortunately he had a persistent skin problem that no cure could be found for. She went on to tell me that: *"unfortunately he has suffered for many years with really severe psoriasis. The condition was so bad his hands were cracked and bleeding and he was pretty much in constant pain. I don't know what made me ask, but I did ask the water elemental if it had any advice about this condition. It instructed me to leave a bottle full of water out for two nights in moonlight and that he should then drink it, a cup per night before retiring. Well, anyway, he was so desperate (after trying all conventional methods without success) he was open to this instruction and duly carried it out. Well, strange to say, his psoriasis has definitely cleared up, the cracks have closed up and the scaly patches greatly faded and he has more use in both hands now!"*

Ways of perceiving the devas

If you want to perceive and connect with the spirits of water, it is something that anyone with sufficient interest and practise can learn to do! You need to give your rational mind a back seat and develop your powers of focussed meditation and visualisation, plus an ability to dowse for energies is also helpful.

To engage the intuitive mind in this quest, find a body of water and relax beside it, eyes closed, clearing your thoughts and sinking deeply into a receptive mode of mind, where brainwaves are much slowed down from normal activity. Then send your mind out into the water, as if you have a blank television screen waiting for a transmission signal. Note anything that might appear on this mind's eye screen, or anything heard.

Alanna's students try water deva dowsing.

Water deva dowsing in Ireland.

Marko Pogacnik suggests another visualisation meditation technique beside a water body, where you imagine that the tail end of your body is turning into a fish tail, or some sort of watery being. Then forget the image and wait for any impressions that comes to mind.

Dowsing for the energy fields that constitute the water spirits is also not particularly difficult. Use remote dowsing to scan around in wet locations for the most powerful and intelligent of any devic energy fields there and find where they are stationed at that moment in time. Introduce yourself and make friends with them. Visit them regularly and give them simple gifts.

How you approach the devas is more important than the method used. Good etiquette goes a long way! The act of asking permission to be able to perceive them and then giving thanks for whatever is received, may well be the key to opening the doors of perception.

A river ritual with friends in Malaysia.

In the process, when we enter that sensitive zone within us we become a receptacle for wisdom. The suite of Cups in the Tarot cards alludes to such intuitive perceptions, the cups bringing us messages and power from other dimensions. It's as if we become a Holy Grail ourselves, tapping into our own inner Davagh's Vat, Brigid's Cauldron of bounty.

Many ways to honour the Spirit of Water

Let's be kind to water! Whether it is a simple expression of thanks to water, or of songs sung to water, whether you simply clean up the rubbish that you find at a local sacred spring that you regularly visit – any and all of these expressions of honouring water are a great gift to the planet. It really doesn't matter how you do it, it is the attitude that you bring to water that matters!

Approach water with a spirit of gratitude. Acts of gifting may be of real life things, or take the form of a visualisation, as purely a thoughtform. For instance, one might visit the local spring and take a flower plucked on the walk there, offering it to the spirits of water, with all your heart. Or simply imagine that you are giving a flower gift!

Another approach is to visit the source of a river and collect a few bottles of its purest waters. Later, when you are downstream, ceremoniously offer this water to the river, to help it maintain its purity. (Such a ritual may be seen in my film 'The Sacred World of Water'.)

On the home front, one might create a sacred water feature in the garden, in a wild space dedicated to nature. Pond and bog gardens can be very beautiful planted out with local aquatic plants and also popular with frogs, fish and insects. It could be a place for you to meditate and a haven for water spirits that you have invited to come and live there. They will be very impressed! But don't employ any metals in deva-friendly landscaping if you want to keep them happy.

Sing and talk to water. Even if it's just water in your tap. The voicing of your love and thanks to water can have powerful resonances throughout nature, as well as to the waters of your own being. It delights the spirits of water and helps to anchor the harmony of place. And, as our bodies are around 70% water, when we love and honour the waters of the planet, we are also taking better care of ourselves!

Through the sacred medium
of water,
our Great Mother,
Let peace, love
and understanding
flow...........

References:

Chapters:
2. Who are the devas and spirits of water?
Gregory, Lady, 'Complete Irish Mythology', Bounty Books 2004, London (originally published 1902).

3. Amphibious creators and storm gods
Jordan, Michael, 'Encyclopaedia of Gods', Kyle Cathie, UK, 2002.
McGrath, Sheena, 'The Sun Goddess', Blandford, UK, 1997.
Hallam, Elizabeth,'Gods and Goddesses' , New Holland, Australia, 1996.
Jordan, Michael, 'Encyclopaedia of the Gods' Kyle Cathie Ltd, UK 1992.

4. Serpent creator spirits
Hodson, Sandra (compiled by), 'Light of the Sanctuary – The Occult Diary of Geoffrey Hodson', Theosophical Publishers, Phillipines, 1988.
Le Quellec, Jean-Loic, trans. P. Bahn (2004), 'Rock Art in Africa: Mythology and Legend', Editions Flammarion, Paris. Via www.sommerland.org
Norman, Neil L and Kelly, Kenneth G, 'Landscape Politics: The Serpent Ditch and the Rainbow in West Africa', The American Anhropologist, 106(1):98-110, 2004.
www.africamissions.org/africa/religion.htm

5. Serpents of Mesopotamia and the Bible
Walker, Barbara, 'The Woman's Encyclopaedia of Myths and Secrets', Harper & Row USA, 1983.

6. Serpents in India and the Americas
Blacker, Carmen and Loewe Micheal, editors,'Ancient Cosmologies' Allen and Unwin, UK, 1975.
Carreon, Hector, 'Strange Rumblings at the Center of our Galaxy', 'La Voz de Aztlan', 2006, www.fourwinds10.com.
'The Eternal Cycle – Indian Myth', Duncan Baird publishers, UK, 1998.
www.en.wikipedia.org/wiki/Quetzalcoatl
Vance, Phil, 'Local Religion and Shrines of Rural India',

www.dragonnetwork.org
'The World of Myths vol 2', British Museum Press, 2004.
Menzies, Jackie et al, 'Goddess – Divine Energy', Art Gallery of NSW, 2006.

7. Chinese snakes and dragons
Storm, Rachel, 'Illustrated Encyclopaedia of Eastern Mythology', Lorenz Books 1999.
Miller, Hamish and Broadhurst, Paul, 'The Sun and the Serpent', Pendragon Press, UK 1989.

8. Serpents and dragons of Europe
Gimbutas, Marija, 'The Goddesses and Gods of Old Europe – Myth and Cult Images 6500 - 3500BC', University of California Press, USA, 1982.

9. The serpent in Ireland
Meehan, Cary, 'The Traveller's Guide to Sacred Ireland', Gothic Image, UK, 2002.
Mac Neill Maire, 'The Festival of Lughnasa', 1962, University College Dublin, Ireland 2008.
Gregory, Lady, 'Visions and Beliefs in the West of Ireland', Colin Smythe Ltd, UK, 1920, 'Complete Irish Mythology' Bounty Books, UK, 1996 (1st ed. 1902).
Holiday, F. W., 'Serpents of the Sky, Dragons of the Earth', Horus House Press, USA, 1973.
Lenihan, Eddie, 'Meeting the Other Crowd – The Fairy Stories of Hidden Ireland', Gill & Macmillan, 2003.
Dames, Michael, 'Mythic Ireland', Thames and Hudson, UK, 1992.

10. Australian Rainbow Serpents
Isaacs, Jennifer, 'Australian Dreaming', Lansdowne Press, Australia, 1980.
Hulley, Charles E, 'The Rainbow Serpent' New Holland, 1999.
Harney, W E (Bill), 'To Ayers Rock and Beyond', Seal Books Rigby Ltd, 1963.
Cairns, Hugh and Harney, Bill Yidumduma 'Dark Sparklers' published by H Cairns, Australia, 2003.
Morrison, Edgar, 'The Loddon Aborigines' self published, Australia, 1971.
Bates, Daisy, 'Aboriginal Perth – Bibbulmun Biographies and Legends' Hesperian Press, Western Australia, 1992.
Barrett, Charles, 'The Bunyip and Other Mythical Monsters and Legends' Reed and Harris, Australia, 1946.

Reed and Harris, Australia, 1946.
'Wurundjeri Dreaming - with Wurundjeri Elder Ian Hunter, on-line.
Hulley, Charles E 'The Rainbow Serpent', New Holland, UK, 1999.
Tully, John, The Mindye Stone Arrangement at Bealiba, Weila Publishing, Australia, 2011.

11. Water and sovereignty goddesses
McMahon, Joanne and Roberts, Jack, 'The Sheela Na Gigs of Ireland and Britain', Mercier Press, 2000, UK.
Kelly, Fergus, 'Early Irish Farming', Dublin Institute for Advanced Studies, 1998.
Monaghan, Patricia, The Book of Goddesses and Heroines, Llewellyn, UK, 1981.
'The Goddess and the Computer', BBC Channel 4, Jan. 1989, via MacUser, January 1989.
'Java's South Sea Goddess', ABC News Online, May 17, 2006
Lie-Birchall, Barrie, 'Parangtritis -A Beach Not Too Far', on-line.
Fitzpatrick, Stephen, 'Disaster strikes at heart of Java identity', The Australian, 29th May 2006.

12. Sun deities and hot springs
Monaghan, Patricia, The Book of Goddesses and Heroines, Llewellyn, UK, 1981.
McGrath, Sheena, The Sun Goddess, Blandford, UK, 1997.

13. Sacred rivers and their deities
Bord, Janet, Cures and Curses – Ritual and Cult at Holy Wells, Heart of Albion Press, UK, 2006.

14. European sirens and nixes
Hodson, Geoffrey, 'Clairvoyant Investigations', Quest, USA, 1984.
Leadbeater, C.W., 'The Hidden Side of Things', Adyer, first published 1913.

15. Water horses
www.mysteriousbritain.co.uk/folklore/eachuisge.html
www.orkneyjar.com/folklore/nokk.htm
/www.romantic-scotland.com/the-water-horse.html
www.druidschool.com/site/1030100/page/891947

16. Lake beings of the world
www.lochness.co.uk

17. Australasian water beings
Cowan , James, 'Maori Folk Tales of the Port Hills', 1923, Whitcombe and Tombs, NZ.
'Art of the Pacific', Oxford University Press, 1979.
Irwin, Rev. J., 'Maori Leviathon', Historical Review, Bay of Plenty Journal of History, vol. 31/2, Nov. 1983.
Best, Simon, 'Here Be Dragons', Journal of Polynesian Society, Sept 1988.
Maddock, Kenneth, 'Taniwha parallels in Australia', Journal of Polynesian Society, Sept. 1988.
Hawkesbury 'Monster' story from 'Windsor and Richmond Gazette' - 8th August, via www.hawkesburyhistory.org.au/stubbs/monster.html

18. Water shrines and healing waters
Jordan, Katy, 'Wells in Depth', The Wellspring, May 2000 (online).
Wilford, John Noble, 'Unearthed: 4600-year-old village of Stonehenge builders', 1-2-07, The Age, Australia.
Bord, Janet, 'Cures and Curses – Ritual and Cult at Holy Wells', Heart of Albion Press, UK, 2006.
Bord, Janet and Colin, 'The Secret Country', Paladin, UK, 1976.
http://www.mysteriousbritain.co.uk
Keegan, Lyn and Keegan Gerald, 'Healing Waters', Berkley Books, USA, 1998.

19. Spirit of Water in Christianity
Sullivan, Danny, Ley Lines – the Greatest Landscape Mystery, Green Magic, UK, 2004.
Condren, Mary, 'The Serpent and the Goddess – Women, Religion and Power in Celtic Ireland', Harper and Row, USA, 1989.
Pennick, Nigel, The Ancient Science of Geomancy', Thames and Hudson, UK.
Screeton, Paul, Quicksilver Heritage, Abacus, UK, 1977.

20. Irish well pilgrimages
O' Cadhla, Stiofan, The Holy Well Tradition, Four Courts Press, Ireland, 2002.
Logan, Patrick, The Holy Wells of Ireland, Colin Smythe, 1980, UK.
Haggerty, Bridget, 'The Holy Wells of Ireland', The Wellspring, online journal.

21. Restoring well traditions in Malvern, England

Rose Garrard, 'Malvern – Hill of Fountains', published by Garrard Art Publications, 2006.

22. The Spirit of Water in today's world

Redgrove, Peter, 'The Black Goddess and the Sixth Sense', Paladin 1989.

Moore, Alanna and Arnold, Billy 'Coogee Beach - Sacred Landscape Temple, A Brief Report of Observations of 'Our Lady of the Fence Posts' site over two years' in Geomantica no. 30, Dec 2005, on-line.

Burke, Kelly, 'The fathers, the sun and the holy post' Sydney Morning Herald, January 31 2003.

Morris, Linda, 'No rest in the quest for Coogee's holy rail' Sydney Morning Herald, February 5, 2005.

24. Honouring water

Moore, Alanna, 'The Wisdom of Water', Python Press, Australia, 2008.

Monaghan, Patricia, 'The Book of Goddesses & Heroines', Llewellyn, UK, 1981.

Emoto, Masaru, 'The Hidden Messages in Water', Simon and Schuster, 2005.

About the Author

Alanna Moore was co-founder of the New South Wales Dowsing Society in 1984 and is now patron of the new Australian Dowsers Society. A professional dowser, internationally known for her writing and teaching of dowsing and geomancy, Alanna lectures worldwide and also makes films. Author of seven books, a permaculture farmer and teacher as well, she disseminates information via her website:

www.geomantica.com

Dowsing Services

Do you sleep in a healthy place? Could there be a sacred site in your back paddock? Where to put a Power Tower to make your garden grow better; or to locate a stone circle site for meditation? And where do the local nature spirits reside? Find out with a geomantic survey by Alanna Moore. House and land surveys available by remote map dowsing to identify areas of noxious or beneficial energy.

Alanna Moore's One Day Workshops

Dowsing for Health – Dowsing the subtle anatomy, health effects of geobiology & electro-biology and how to avoid it, remote analysis and healing.

Sacred Garden – How to harness subtle energies for enhanced plant growth and animal wellbeing. Geomantic, sensitive permaculture design.

Divining Earth Harmony – Geomancy, building biology, map dowsing, Earth acupuncture & other Earth harmony techniques.

Deva Dowsing – Connecting energetically with the Earth and its devic beings, landscape geomancy and Earth ritual.

Correspondence Course:

Diploma of Dowsing for Harmony

Since 1989 this course has allowed students to learn gradually, at their own pace in their own home, paying as they go (10 payments of $55).

Start whenever you like, $100 off for full payment in advance ($450).

Comprehensive notes and dowsing exercises from Australia's most experienced dowsing teacher, Alanna Moore.

Geomantica Films

by Alanna Moore

Only available from Geomantica.com

See excerpts at Geomantica Films on YouTube.

The ART of DOWSING & GEOMANCY

140 minutes of dowsing and geomancy training sessions. Be a fly on the wall watching Alanna Moore as she teachs students.
Ideal for beginners.

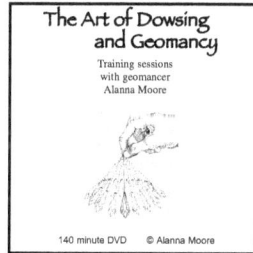

The Art of Dowsing and Geomancy
Training sessions with geomancer Alanna Moore

140 minute DVD   © Alanna Moore

Dowsers Down Under

Seven master dowsers around Australia talk about their experiences with water, opal and gold divining, map dowsing, health divination, radionic healing, Earth acupuncture, finding lost graves of Ned Kelly's bushranger gang, soil testing, blink dowsing, and much more!

DVD 102 mins.

What reviewers have said of Dowsers Down Under:

"If you are interested in dowsing, then may I strongly suggest you get hold of this video; it is very informative" - Duncan Roads, Nexus, June/July 2002.

"This really is a tremendous video" - Dowsers Society of NSW

Three documentary film series
by Alanna Moore:

EARTH CARE, EARTH REPAIR film series

Each film around half an hour.

Part 1: **Dowsing, Greening & Crystal Farming**- Using dowsing in the garden.

Part 2: **Eco-Gardeners Down-Under** - Permaculture pioneers Bill Mollison, David Holmgren and Jane Lawrance interviewed, you'll see their gardens too.

Part 3: **Grassroots Solutions for Soil Salinity** - Radical farmers and a water scientist explain dryland salinity and successes in saving soils that rely on dowsing are showcased.

Earth Care
Earth Repair

film series
parts 7 & 8:

AGNIHOTRA
- HOMA FARMING

RADIONIC FARMING & LANDCARE
IN AUSTRALASIA

PAL DVD
75 mins
© Alanna Moore 2004
www.geomantica.com
Geomantica PO Box 929 Castlemaine 3450 Vic Australia

Part 4: **Growing & Gauging Sustainability** - From tapping into Universal Knowledge in farming, to gauging success in sustainable growing.

Part 5: **Remineralising the Soil** - The fertilising value of volcanic rock dust and how it can save our soils. It's got great energy as well!

Part 6: **Making Power Towers** - A look at Irish Round Towers and their modern counterparts, the Towers of Power, for enhancing plant growth.

Part 7: **Agnihotra / Homa Farming** - Ancient vedic fire rituals have been revived for a renaisssance in agriculture that also heals the land and people.

Part 8: **Radionic Farming & Landcare** - Advanced dowsing techniques, known as radionics, offer esoteric alternatives to unsustainable agriculture. See special coils on farms designed to spread beneficial energies.

GEOMANCY TODAY film series

Each film around half an hour.

Part 1: **Megalithomania** - A look at the fascination with megalithic monuments, especially standing stones, stone circles and labyrinths; their energetic features and how to make your own for ritual use.

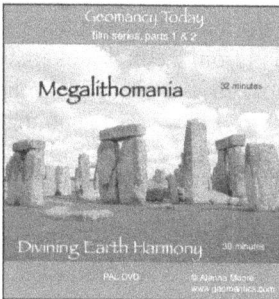

Part 2: **Divining Earth Harmony** - A look at feng shui, plus geomancers talking about their Earth harmonising work.

Part 3: **Discovering the Devas** - Who are the spirits of nature and where to find them today.

Part 4: **Helping the Devas** - Swedish dowsers who specialise in helping the forest devas (trolls) explain how devas need our help.

Part 5: **The Sacred World of Water** - This film compliments the book Water Spirits of the World

STATE of PILGRIMAGE film series

Each film around half an hour.

Part 1: **Glastonbell Dreaming** - Australia's first white geomancer talks of his quest for the sacred in the Blue Mountains of New South Wales.

Part 2: **Pilgrimage to Central Australia** - Travelling through Central Australia with clairvoyant seers one is introduced to the spiritual reality of the Aboriginal Dreamtime & vibrant indigenous culture.

Part 3: **A Thirst for Ireland** - A search for Irish roots reveals that the Celtic Dreamtime in the Emerald Isle is alive as well!

Part 4: **Saving Tara** - The foremost of Irelands sacred sites is threatened by a motorway development, protestors explain its significance and a Druid reveals the role of the Opus Dei in its destruction.

Part 5: **South Australian Sojourn** - From the rich delta of the Murray River to Adelaide's festivals and the mysterious Flinders Ranges - some of SA's geomantic features are revealed.

Part 6: **Bali - geomantic journeying in paradise** - A geomancers delight, Bali has strong geomantic traditions and powerful energies associated with its sacred volcanoes and lakes. Colourful rituals complement the tropical intensity; and rules of village and household layout are explained.

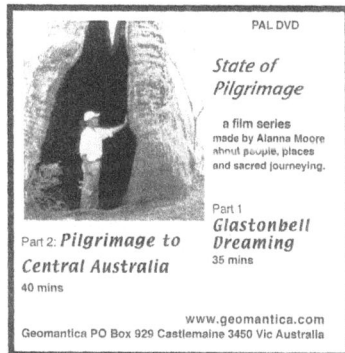

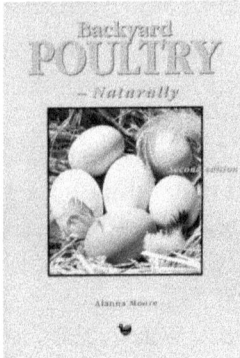

Backyard Poultry - Naturally

From housing to feeding, from selection to breeding, from pets to production and from the best lookers to the best layers, this book covers everything the backyard farmer needs to know about poultry husbandry - including preventative and curative herbal medicines and homeopathics, plus permaculture design for poultry pens.

The Reviews:

"A wonderful resource! Alanna Moore has provided poultry enthusiasts with all the information they need to raise healthy poultry without using harmful chemicals."
Megg Miller, Grass Roots magazine.

"The poultry health section is the best I've seen."
Eve Sinton, Permaculture International Journal.

"An interesting and worthwhile book that will no doubt have a lot of appeal for the amateur or part-time farmer."
Kerry Lonergan, Landline, ABC TV.

Stone Age Farming
- Tapping nature's subtle energies for your farm or garden

From Irish Round Towers to modern Towers of Power for enhancing plant growth. In this book ancient and modern ideas about the energies of rocks are explored for practical application in the garden.

This new 2nd edition has been revised and updated ten years after the first, in 2011.

What reviewers said of the 1st edition:

"Simply fabulous!" M. Finkel, Health and Healing.
"Quite fantastic."
Roberta Britt, Canadian Quester Journal.

"Clear, lucid and practical" Tom Graves
"A classic" Radionics Network.

"Will change your perception of the world"
Conscious Living magazine.

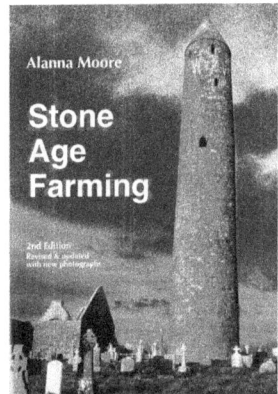

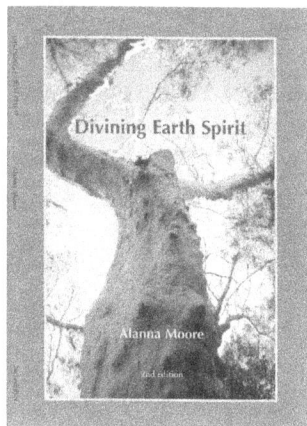

Divining Earth Spirit
- An Exploration of Global & Australasian Geomancy

A comprehensive look at the many aspects of geomancy and geobiology.

What reviewers have said of it:

"This book is a classic for anyone wanting to get involved with Earth healing. It contains information by the bucketload... The research that has gone into this book is incredible and no doubt will stir you into wanting to use it yourself."
Radionics Network Vol. 2 No.6

"Excellent reference book"

Don McLeod, Silver Wheel

"Love of the topic clearly shows, as Moore brings clarity and a sense of the necessity of personal involvement and engagement with the Earth. The great advantage of Moore's book is in its detailing all the salient aspects of Earth Spirit phenomena....all covered succinctly and with precision... the perfect introduction to the topic," Esoterica magazine, No. 4, 1995

"Highly recommended" Glastonbell Vol. 5 No 4

The Magic of Menhirs and Circles of Stone

Discover the world of standing stones, stone circles, medicine wheels and labyrinths. How to make them and utilise them for improved Earth harmony and personal benefits. Includes recent energetic investigations of these Earth mysteries by dowsers.

"Have you ever wanted a sacred site in your own back yard? This book will help you to achieve that dream."

Don McLeod in 'Silver Wheel', SA.

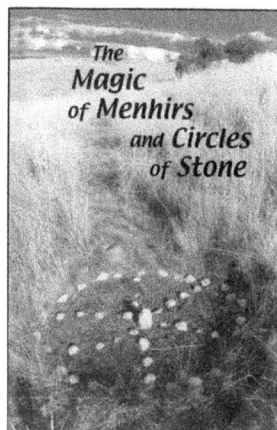

The Wisdom of Water

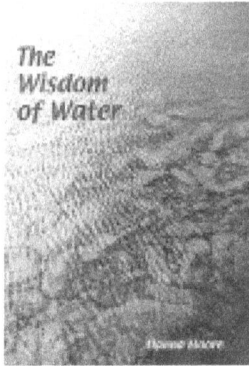

Water tends to vanish when human impacts are high. But we can reverse the trend and reconnect with the wisdom and healing powers of water.

In this 2007 book Alanna Moore delves into water's mysterious origins and manifestations; its energetic and spiritual aspects; global traditions; as well as water in Australian landscapes.

The potential of water divining, and 'new' water (created deep within the Earth) provides hope for a sustainable, water-secure future, she believes.

What has been said of this book:
"Very invigorating. Highly recommended"
Jilli Roberts, Pagan Times Dec 2007

"A great book!" Professor Stuart Hill

Sensitive Permaculture
- cultivating the way of the sacred Earth

This 2009 book explores the living energies of the land and how to sensitively connect with them. Positive and joyful, it draws on the indigenous wisdom of Australasia, Ireland and elsewhere, combining the insights of geomancy and geobiology with eco-smart permaculture design to offer an exciting new paradigm for sustainable living. It includes the authors experiences of negotiating with fairy beings and dragon spirits over land use in Australia and Ireland and, as in the co-creative gardening at Scotland's Findhorn community, there's a giant cabbage in there too!

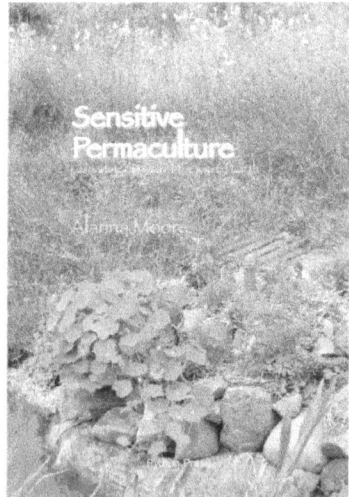

www.ingramcontent.com/pod-product-compliance
Lightning Source LLC
Chambersburg PA
CBHW072139020426
42334CB00018B/1855